Developing an Integrated Delivery System

Organizing a Seamless System of Care

APA PRACTITIONER'S TOOLBOX SERIES

BUILDING A GROUP PRACTICE: CREATING A SHARED VISION FOR SUCCESS

CONTRACTING ON A CAPITATED BASIS: MANAGING RISK FOR YOUR PRACTICE

CONTRACTING WITH ORGANIZATION DELIVERY SYSTEMS: SELECTING, EVALUATING, AND NEGOTIATING CONTRACTS

DEVELOPING AN INTEGRATED DELIVERY SYSTEM: ORGANIZING A SEAMLESS SYSTEM OF CARE

MANAGING YOUR PRACTICE FINANCES: STRATEGIES FOR BUDGETING, FUNDING, AND BUSINESS PLANNING

MARKETING YOUR PRACTICE: CREATING OPPORTUNITIES FOR SUCCESS

MODELS FOR MULTIDISCIPLINARY ARRANGEMENTS: A STATE-BY-STATE REVIEW OF OPTIONS

ORGANIZING YOUR PRACTICE THROUGH AUTOMATION: MANAGING INFORMATION AND DATA

PRACTICING OUTSIDE OF THIRD-PARTY REIMBURSEMENT: DIVERSIFYING FOR YOUR FUTURE

APA Practitioner's Toolbox Series

Developing an Integrated Delivery System

Organizing a Seamless System of Care

American Psychological Association Practice Directorate
with
Coopers & Lybrand, L.L.P.

AMERICAN PSYCHOLOGICAL ASSOCIATION
Washington, DC

A Cautionary Note:

This manual was written to serve both as a reference and as a tool to help providers practice more efficiently in a changing, demanding marketplace. The information contained herein is accurate and complete to the best of our knowledge. However, *Developing an Integrated Delivery System: Organizing a Seamless System of Care* should be read with the understanding that it is meant as a supplement, not a substitute, for sound legal, accounting, business, or other professional consulting services. When such services are required, the assistance of a competent professional should be sought.

Copyright © 1996 by the American Psychological Association.
All rights reserved. Except as permitted under the United States Copyright Act of 1976, no part of this publication may be reproduced or distributed in any form or by any means, or stored in a database or retrieval system, without the prior written permission of the publisher.

Published by
American Psychological Association
750 First Street, NE
Washington, DC 20002

Copies may be ordered from
APA Order Department
P.O. Box 2710
Hyattsville, MD 20784

Composition and Printing: National Academy Press, Washington, DC
Cover Designer: Leigh Coriale

Library of Congress Cataloging-in-Publication Data
Developing an integrated delivery system: organizing a seamless system of care / American Psychological Association Practice Directorate with Coopers & Lybrand, L.L.P.
    p. cm. — (APA practitioner's toolbox series)
  Includes bibliographical references.
  ISBN 1-55798-350-X (alk. paper)
  1. Clinical psychology—Practice—United States. 2. Managed mental health care—United States. 3. Integrated delivery of health care—United States. I. American Psychological Association. Practice Directorate. II. Coopers & Lybrand. III. Series. [DNLM: 1. Delivery of Health Care, Integrated—organization & administration. 2. Mental Health Services—organization & administration. W 84.1 D488 1996]
  RC467.95.D48 1996
  362.2'0973—dc20
  DLM/DLC
  for Library of Congress
                                                  95-4648
                                                      CIP

British Library Cataloguing-In-Publication Data
A CIP record is available from the British Library

Printed in the United States of America
First Edition

Contents

FOREWORD FROM RUSS NEWMAN, PHD, JD · vii

PREFACE · ix
    The Evolving Market for Behavioral Health Care Services
    Development of New Delivery Systems
    How to Use This Guidebook

ACKNOWLEDGMENTS · xv

PART I: BACKGROUD AND CONCEPTS · 1

1 UNDERSTANDING INTEGRATION · 3
    Market Forces Encourage Change / 3
    Integration as a Strategy for Control / 8
    Summary / 9
    Case Study / 10

2 HORIZONTAL INTEGRATION · 11
    What Is Horizontal Integration? / 11
    Why Consider Horizontal Integration? / 12
    Models for Horizontal Integration / 14
    The Process of Horizontal Integration / 18
    Some Caveats to Horizontal Integration / 21
    Summary / 23
    Case Study / 23

3 VERTICAL INTEGRATION · 25
    Vertical Integration / 25
    Market Strategy / 26

PHO Models / 29
PHO Governance / 31
Clinical Management / 32
Summary / 34
Case Study / 35

4　FULLY INTEGRATED DELIVERY SYSTEMS　　36
Market Dominance / 36
IDS Models / 38
Summary / 41
Case Study / 41

PART II: HOW TO BUILD AND INTEGRATED DELIVERY SYSTEM　　43

5　ACHIEVING INTEGRATION　　45
Federal Scrutiny of Providers / 45
Tax Status / 47
Governance Structure / 51
Other Legal Concerns / 54
Scope of Services Offered / 55
Network Hospitals / 57
Providers / 58
Other Health Care Providers / 59
Summary / 59
Case Study / 60

6　INFRASTRUCTURE NEEDS FOR INTEGRATION　　61
Administrative Structure / 61
Clinical Management / 69
Information Systems / 70
Budget Projections / 73
Third Party Administration / 74
Outside Assistance / 74
Case Study / 76

GLOSSARY　　77

BIBLIOGRAPHY　　84

AMERICAN
PSYCHOLOGICAL
ASSOCIATION

Dear Colleague:

The American Psychological Association is pleased to offer <u>Developing an Integrated Delivery System: Organizing a Seamless System of Care</u> as one component of the "APA Practitioner's Toolbox Series" written in conjunction with Coopers & Lybrand, L.L.P. This series of educational tools is designed to help psychologists build successful practices in an increasingly complex environment while maintaining the quality that has become the hallmark of psychological services.

Over the past 15 to 20 years, the healthcare marketplace has witnessed tremendous integration and consolidation. The quest for administrative cost savings and greater efficiency in the delivery of services, as well as the increase in "corporatized" healthcare, have driven the process. The evolution of managed care has been both a byproduct of the growing corporatization and another factor increasing the integration of services. Recent federal and state efforts to reform the healthcare delivery system have been consistent with the drive towards seamless and integrated systems of healthcare.

An initial step for practitioners, in an effort to keep pace with this integration, is the formation of group practices, the subject the "APA Practitioner's Toolbox Series" book <u>Building a Group Practice: Creating a Shared Vision for Success</u>. Much further down the integration continuum is the establishment of integrated delivery systems (IDSs) -- strategic alliances of providers and hospitals who assume shared risk for the purposes of ownership, capital, financing, governance, and management. An IDS attempts to provide the purchaser or consumer of behavioral healthcare access to a broad range of services through a central source, or a "one-stop-shop" approach to healthcare in an effort to maximize efficiency.

One strategy for maximizing provider decision making and control over services in the increasingly integrated health system is to develop provider-driven integrated delivery systems. It is here that psychologists can participate in the development of mechanisms which not only provide a wide range of services, but also increase our ability to determine when, how, and by whom psychological services are delivered. This manual is intended to help those providers wishing to employ this strategy for dealing with the changing healthcare environment.

Sincerely,

Russ Newman, Ph.D., J.D.
Executive Director for Professional Practice

750 First Street, NE
Washington, DC 20002-4242
(202) 336-5913
(202) 336-5797 Fax
(202) 336-6123 TDD

Russ Newman, Ph.D., J.D.
Executive Director
Practice Directorate

Preface

Practitioners face new challenges resulting from health-care market-reform initiatives that make it increasingly difficult to rely upon the skills and strategies that have served so well in the past. In addition to our continued advocacy against the threats of short-sighted efforts that sacrifice quality and outcomes for temporary cost-savings, psychologists have an opportunity to develop and use the substantial bargaining power that can be achieved through our collective creativity and energy. One mechanism for joining together is the development of integrated delivery systems, provider-driven organizations that include a full continuum of caregivers.

The APA Practitioner's Toolbox Series is dedicated to the concept that by becoming better informed about the market changes occurring in health care today, we can develop strategies to preserve the quality of care in spite of economic necessities and choose to participate in systems that recognize that the distinction between low cost and high value is the quality and outcome of care. Ultimately, those systems that deny access to needed services in the name of cost control cannot succeed. Care may be postponed temporarily, but only at an ever-increasing total cost that must eventually be paid.

Each of the topics included in the APA Practitioner's Toolbox Series has been selected because of an increasing volume of requests received for information on the topic. Taken together, the manuals may assist the practitioner in channeling energy into a constructive strategy for achieving the goal of preserving quality in an evolving health care market.

THE EVOLVING MARKET FOR BEHAVIORAL HEALTH CARE SERVICES

Although comprehensive national health reform died in the halls of Congress in 1994, market reform continues to occur. The health care industry is characterized by rapid change in the delivery and reimbursement of care. This is in part driven by increased sophistication in purchasing strategies of payers and insurers, who demand more efficient and appropriate delivery of behavioral health care services. The psychologist who understands market reform may develop an effective business strategy that increases provider control of the clinical and economic aspects of the practice.

The 1980s and the early 1990s were characterized by unprecedented growth in the delivery of psychiatric and chemical dependency care. The number of private, free-standing psychiatric and chemical dependency hospitals more than doubled, while the number of medical surgical hospitals offering psychiatric/chemical dependency care increased more than 25%.

Corresponding to this growth, employers, insurance companies, and other payers saw their year-to-year costs for behavioral health care increase at a rate that more than doubled the Medical Consumer Price Index. Companies reported that behavioral health costs had grown to 15% to 25% of their total costs for health care, with some reporting costs beyond 25%. In response to these cost pressures, many employers and insurance companies began implementing managed care initiatives. In many markets, "managed" behavioral health care is aggressively pursued.

Managed care is a means of providing health care services within a defined network of health care providers who are given the responsibility to manage and provide quality, cost-effective care. Historically, behavioral health care admissions have been defined by the provider of record, who determined the intensity and length of care. The advent of managed care changed this by implementing protocols that define admission criteria and period of confinement. No longer is the individual psychologist, in coordination with the patient and the treating facility, the sole determiner of treatment.

In times past, the medical economics of patient care was characterized by the psychologist and patient agreeing on a course of treatment, with payment being the responsibility of employers and insurance companies, resulting in an unrestrained level of demand for care and services. Ultimately, uncontrolled increases in health care costs stimulated the implementation of managed care, which changed the treatment decision process by inserting the payer as a third party. Payers have, therefore, demanded reduced costs, shorter lengths of stay, and new modes of care. As the market continues its reform, providers increasingly are required to deliver services along the behavioral health "continuum of care," generally defined as inpatient residential treatment, partial hospitalization, home health, and outpatient services. Payers are increasingly requiring that psychologists practice along this continuum.

In general, the market has explored various methods to control health care costs. Approaches that have been used extensively include cost controls (e.g., negotiated reduced rates, capitation payments, fee schedules, per diem payments, and prospectively set prices based on diagnoses) and utilization controls (e.g., precertification, second opinion, utilization review requirements, case management, and discharge planning.) Cost controls tend to be financial agreements that do not involve the payer in treatment decisions made by providers. Utilization controls may influence treatment decisions since they monitor care, attempting to ensure that only appropriate psychologically and medically necessary care is being provided. Utilization controls also strive to ensure that care is delivered by the provider at the most appropriate level of care.

This continual evolution on the part of the health care community to contain and, in fact, lower costs has met with mixed results. Within the last decade, payers of care have opted to place providers "at risk" for the delivery of their services, that is, each provider or system of care is prepaid for all services and required to provide care within a fixed budget.

One of the single largest dynamics in the evolving health care market is the assumption of financial risk by the providers of care. Managed care has ushered in an era in which the lines between insurer and provider are not well delineated, since both assume financial risk under certain conditions. Assumption of risk for services occurs at all levels in the delivery system, although its form varies from market to market.

Capitation

In a capitated system, a provider or group of providers agrees (within defined parameters) to deliver all of the behavioral health services required by a given population for a fixed cost per member. In this system, providers assume financial risk for a given population because payment to the provider is the same regardless of the amount or cost of care rendered. In capitated contracting, the unit of service is the covered life (member).

DEVELOPMENT OF NEW DELIVERY SYSTEMS

Throughout the market, creative providers are organizing themselves to effectively deliver behavioral health care within systems of care. The result of this reorganization, and rethinking, about health care services is the emergence of the integrated delivery systems (IDSs). These systems offer "one-stop shopping" to potential payers, meaning that a payer can write "one check" for the entire delivery of mental health care for its employees without having to negotiate terms with multiple, unconnected providers. IDSs offer a full continuum of care so that patients (and premiums) are managed within one accountable plan's network of providers. In theory, IDSs provide easy access, coordinate the continuity of care, quantify and standardize quality, reduce clinical and administrative redundancy, align provider incentives (practitioner and hospital), and provide for easier contracting and marketing to third-party payers. The individual practitioner may find that life within an IDS may be more regulated than private practice with committee-developed standards of care, policies, procedures and protocols. Along with a loss of autonomy at the individual level, however, comes an increased opportunity to participate in development of protocols for other practitioners, including, for example, setting clinical parameters for primary care physicians for the appropriate treatment of depression. Additionally, the practitioner may be relieved of some business risk, such as making the payroll for office staff; he or she will assume increased accountability for outcomes with practices profiles, peer norm comparisons, and other measurements of clinical performance used by an IDS.

This book was developed to assist the psychologist in making such a move. As a guidebook, it first discusses horizontal integration with other behavioral health practitioners over a geographical area as a means for achieving increased bargaining clout. Then, vertical integration is discussed to control the continuum of care and reduce costs, and, ultimately, development of a fully integrated system of care with equity participation by the psychologist is discussed. Along the way, alternative destinations are considered, with a rationale developed for each recommended route.

For those psychologists satisfied with the role of provider, the guidebook offers insight into changes occurring in the health care system that may ultimately have repercussions in behavioral health care and offers some advice on dealing with specific managed care initiatives. The primary audience for this guidebook, however, is the practitioner who wants to take an active role in designing the delivery system for care as opposed to accepting managed care initiatives designed to control the delivery of care.

HOW TO USE THIS GUIDEBOOK

This guidebook is designed to help the psychologist organize his or her delivery of behavioral health care services as a means for maintaining or regaining control over the therapeutic decision-making process. As a by-product, the psychologist may expect to achieve financial rewards, but financial power is not usually the goal for integration of service delivery. The goal is practitioner control of decisions that affect client and patient lives. The objective is protection of the therapeutic relationship that exists between the therapist and the client.

The book is divided into two sections. Part I covers the background information and concepts necessary to develop an IDS. The potential threats to the relationship between client and therapist are the subject of chapter 1, in that an environmental assessment overviews the managed care environment, market forces, and practitioner choices. Through horizontal integration, the practitioner can ensure that managed care organizations listen to concerns about ethics, professionalism, and quality. "United we stand, divided we fall" is the rally cry of horizontal integration, discussed in chapter 2. Expansion into the continuum of care is the subject of chapter 3, Vertical Integration, that explores the concept of leverage and substitution theory. In chapter 4, the relationship between a fully integrated system of care and the psychologist is examined to determine a model that respects the practitioner's relationship with the client.

Part II of the book covers how to build an integrated delivery system. Chapters 5 and 6 outline specific details to be considered in forming an integrated delivery system. Obviously, this guide cannot substitute for competent legal counsel, financial advice, and other consulting assistance. However, it can serve as a model process for developing and implementing an integration strategy.

Acknowledgments

This book and associated software were written by Alfred E. Schellhorn, MBA, of Coopers & Lybrand LLP. Mr Schellhorn is a consultant with Coopers & Lybrand's Health and Welfare Practice in Atlanta.

The following individuals from both the American Psychological Association and Coopers & Lybrand were instrumental in providing editorial assistance toward the successful completion of this work:

American Psychological Association
Russ Newman, PhD, JD
C. Henry Engleka
Stuart Koman, PhD
Chris Vein
Craig Olswang
Neela Agarwalla, JD
Garth Huston

Coopers & Lybrand, L.L.P
Ronald A. Finch, EdD
Wanda Bishop

PART I

Background and Concepts

1

Understanding Integration

TO SET A STAGE FOR MEANINGFUL *discussion of integrated delivery systems, this chapter explores the market forces contributing to provider consolidation and the various factors that combine to create those market forces. With this information, providers may better choose how to respond to these market forces. The chapter also introduces some of the terms used throughout the text.*

MARKET FORCES ENCOURAGE CHANGE

Frequent news of mergers and acquisitions among providers, payers, and related organizations is an indication of major market change occurring in America's health care delivery system. Consolidations have resulted from the need of payers to control costs. Providers may also choose to consolidate because of market pressures to improve service, reduce costs, and accept accountability. These pressures have been created not by the consumers of health care, the patients, but by the payer community, including federal and state governments, insurance companies, and employers. Responding to the increased administrative demands of modern health care has been a daunting task for the solo practitioner. Consolidation with other health care providers may ease the practitioner's transition into the managed care environment, substantially improve the odds of success in the new market place, and assist with meeting these new demands on practice time and skills.

The three market pressure categories mentioned above can be divided into component factors—improved service, reduced costs, and financial

TABLE 1 Responses to a Changing Market

Improve Service	Reduce Costs	Accept Accountability
Demonstrate value: • Collect clinical data on outcomes of treatment • Adjust outcomes data for severity • Measure customer satisfaction • Compile encounter statistics • Benchmark results	**Utilize leverage:** • Perform triage review • Direct patients to lowest cost providers • Avoid acute admissions	**Performance contracts:** • Contract renewals contingent upon performance outcomes measurement, bonus incentives
Document competence: • Credential care givers • Profile performance indicators • Monitor compliance with treatment protocols • Benchmark results by provider type	**Reduce excess capacity:** • Project care needs • Limit number of providers based on projection of needs	**Share risk:** • Create withhold pools • Take bonus instead of salary • Contract for flat fee • Contract for capitated rate
Monitor access: • Measure waiting times • Calculate driving distance to nearest provider • Ratio providers to members	**Eliminate redundancy:** • Integrate systems • Collect data only once • Share infrastructures	

accountability—that may be more familiar to the practitioner. These factors are outlined in Table 1 and discussed below.

Improved Service

Providers are being asked to demonstrate quality of care and efficiency of care delivery. Demonstrating value may require comparison with other providers, which, in turn, requires severity adjustment of outcomes data. Providers face increasing demands for documentation of competence in terms of profiles and report cards that compare each practitioner to a peer group or other norm. Providers are asked to produce periodic data monitoring client access, including geographic dispersion and delays in scheduling appointments.

Reduced Costs

Providers are expected to channel patients in the system through triage and needs assessment processes—in essence, creating systems that ensure patients are referred to the lowest level of care appropriate for their condition. Providers are also being pressured to limit capacity to the number of practitioners and acute care beds to the level of projected need. Providers are asked to eliminate redundancy in the delivery process by sharing administrative infrastructures.

Financial Accountability

Providers are asked to accept incentive contracts that place reimbursement at risk for meeting specified performance expectations.

As a result, the delivery of health care is undergoing a major reorganization that has the potential to affect every provider and practitioner in America. To best understand the systemic changes occurring, the key market demands—leverage, value and risk—may warrant review.

Leverage. One of the key principles of cost management in health care has been leverage. By reducing the level of care, a payer reduces its costs, *all other variables remaining equal*. The payer's medical management function exists for the purpose of diverting patients to the lowest cost provider who can be expected to fulfill the patient's needs. In general, the payer is concerned with cost and quality of care—the type of provider is immaterial. This concept is especially important in behavioral health where numerous substitutes exist.

Counseling and therapy services can be provided by a variety of practitioners. In many markets, clinical social workers, psychiatric nurses, marriage and family counselors, and other professional counselors accept fees competitive with those of psychologists whose fees are generally very close to those of psychiatrists. Therefore, payers push for the least costly practitioner to provide the services on the *assumption* that all other variables are equal. Operationally, if medication or hospitalization is indicated in the initial triage process, the patient may be referred to a psychiatrist (depending on state law). If not, referral may be made to a less costly alternative.

One way for psychologists to challenge this process is to demonstrate that other variables are *not* equal. Cost is a function not only of the fee per session but also the number of sessions and the outcome of treatment. Recidivism rates, subsequent admissions, and additional medical costs for pain relievers, sleeping pills, and anti-depressants, just to name a few, can quickly offset the payer's "savings." In fact, the concept of "medical offset" is gaining acceptance among payers and employers. If a practitioner can demonstrate that a difference in outcomes or duration exists when a substitute is utilized to provide treatment, the payer can be expected to act upon that information in its own best interest by developing treatment protocols that direct patients to the most cost effective provider. Obviously, this challenge assumes the practitioner has information available to demonstrate value.

Value. Defined as the ratio of quality to cost, value is the balance of service, access, convenience, quality, satisfaction, and outcome against cost. Beginning in the mid 1960s, the focus of health care policy in America was on improving health through greater access to care. In the late 1980s, the emphasis shifted to control of costs, often without adequate regard for quality, service, access, or outcome. In the mid 1990s, a more balanced principle is emerging to guide policy and decision makers—value-based purchasing. The basic tenets of value-based purchasing permit subjective and objective analysis of alternatives. When purchasing an automobile, the consumer establishes a list of buying criteria that may include subjective opinions (e.g., sportiness) and objective assessments (e.g., two air bags) in addition to price. Similarly, when a health care payer seeks to contract with a provider, the buying criteria are no longer limited to fees.

Payers who are converting to value-based purchasing are demanding new information from practitioners, information that may not be readily available or sufficiently accurate to support decision making. Information requested by payers might include:

- recidivism rates for selected conditions
- duration of treatment for specified conditions
- total treatment costs for an episode of care (including costs for inpatient, outpatient, and medications and all providers seen)

Compliance with these data requests can be problematic for a small group or solo practitioner without sophisticated computer support and a flair for data analysis. One mechanism for responding to these new market expectations is to join with other practitioners in developing systems and processes that support data collection and reporting. Integration, however, invariably results in some loss of practice autonomy in exchange for data compliance. For example, all practitioners may be required to use the same form to record patient diagnosis, treatment, and encounter data. For small groups and solo practitioners, there are two choices: invest in the necessary reporting systems, or forego the payer's business. Ultimately, the market may reach a saturation point where payers have contracted with a sufficient number of practitioners to meet demand projections and freeze the number of providers in their networks.

Risk. In addition to value-based purchasing, many payers are now shifting financial risk to providers. Initially, such shifts centered on withhold pools whereby the payer held back a certain percentage of the normal payment amount until the end of the year. Incentive bonuses were paid for meeting specified performance goals, and global or bundled fees in which the provider agreed to accept a flat amount per admission or other defined episode of care dependent upon the patient's condition became prevalent. More recently, payers have been entering into capitation agreements with providers in which payment is made regardless of patient condition, utilization, or need. Capitation agreements reverse the provider's incentives: the practitioner's profit is diminished with each additional unit of service provided. Therefore, it is in the practitioner's best financial interest to control utilization and manage care in the least restrictive and most appropriate environment. The formidable restraining forces, of course, are legal liability for care of the patient and provision of services within acceptable ethical standards.

Capitation payments are routinely made at the beginning of each month, in advance of service delivery, based upon membership records as of the middle of the prior month. Therefore, practitioners can expect significant improvement in their cash flow. In fact, the revenue may be sufficient to cover all administrative overhead costs for the month, relieving the practitioner of the stress associated with "making the payroll."

The actual capitation payment amount is the product of the number of enrolled members and a per member per month (PMPM) dollar amount. The capitation rate may be computed by a health care actuary (employed by either the payer or the practitioner) who bases payment upon extensive analysis of historical claims experience data. Whenever possible, data needs to be specific to the population to be served, include three years' history, and contain demographic information for each patient (age, sex, and membership basis). Capitation rates are extremely variable in behavioral health care depending on the services included in the rate, competition in the market, and strength of utilization controls applied as described in detail in the APA Practitioner's Toolbox Series volume *Contracting on a Capitated Basis: Managing Risk for Your Practice.*

It may prove useful for psychologists to review the underlying assumptions made by a payer's actuary to confirm their accuracy and validity. For example, the actuary may be using a commercially insured population that is younger than appropriate for the group. An especially important assumption affecting capitated rate calculations is that the provider will serve a sufficient number of members. Serving a very small number of members does not give the provider a chance for utilization to "average out" their risks. In other words, acceptance of a capitation rate as payment may present a higher than average risk for the individual practitioner because adverse selection and high cost "outliers" may occur. Therefore, integration is one means for developing the critical mass necessary to reduce risk.

INTEGRATION AS A STRATEGY FOR CONTROL

Integration implies a strategic alliance or alignment for a specified purpose, such as increased name recognition, bargaining power, market clout, or improved access to capital. Traditionally, three types of itegration exist:

Horizontal

Joining with others who provide the same or similar services is horizontal integration. Geographic alliances and group practices are the most common forms of horizontal integration but alternatives exist that may offer greater autonomy to the solo practitioner.

Vertical

Uniting with providers who are not direct competitors is vertical integration. A provider-hospital organization (PHO) is one example of a vertically integrated network where the strategic alliance is formed between providers and hospitals for the purpose of providing, for example, both inpatient and outpatient services.

Full

Joining a "seamless" delivery system with the features of both horizontal and vertical integration is full integration. A health maintenance organization (HMO) might be an example of a fully integrated delivery system for medical care.

These three options are explored in some detail in later chapters. The order of presentation is significant to the practitioner. Because it may be easier to align initially with other professionals with similar training, experience, and values, horizontal integration is presented first. Additionally, horizontally integrated networks of practitioners may be in an enhanced position of strength in negotiating vertical integration agreements.

Both horizontally and vertically integrated networks are transitional organizations, stepping stones, if you will, to full-fledged IDSs. With its ability to align the incentives of various provider types and groups, the IDS is in the theoretically best position to streamline costs and achieve a competitive advantage in the market over less "evolved" networks. Therefore, the IDS is expected to become more frequent in the market over the next decade.

Joining or forming an integrated network offers several advantages to the practitioner:

Marketing. Most networks assist or perform marketing services on behalf of their members—freeing the practitioner to focus on treatment and clinical responsibilities.

Administrative. By sharing the overhead costs of reception, billing, purchasing, and computer systems, practitioners may achieve economies of scale.

Bargaining Clout. Negotiations with large payers favor a network of providers.

Financial Strength. A network can raise capital more easily than an individual.

Peer Support. Access to specialists and colleagues is enhanced through networking.

Although an integration strategy may not be appropriate for all psychologists, payer demand warrants consideration of the possible advantages to be achieved through alliances with other practitioners.

SUMMARY

The three major market forces that combine to encourage integration among providers are demands to improve service through increased monitoring of satisfaction, outcomes, and access; to reduce costs by steering patients to lowest cost providers, reducing capacity, and eliminating administrative redundancies, and to accept financial accountability through risk and incentive contracts. Integration may be an effective strategy not only for responding to these market pressures, but also for maintaining the psychologist's control of decision making.

CASE STUDY

Specializing in marriage and family counseling, Cheryl Logan, PhD, is well respected in the mental and behavioral health community, not only as a clinician but also as an entrepreneur. Her private practice has grown over the past twelve years to include four professional staff and three administrative staff members. She serves on the Board of United Way, helped to create the local women's shelter, and does a monthly guest commentary on a local news program. Cheryl has consulting staff privileges at two hospitals, is on the Medicare and Blue Cross provider panel, and has an employee assistance program contract with a key employer in the community.

She has developed a successful market strategy that focuses on building strong relationships with her referral sources. Recently, she has been informed by three physician providers who have been loyal referral sources that the managed care contracts they signed require them to refer their patients to another provider. Although each offered to sponsor her for the provider panel of the managed care organizations, Cheryl's response was guarded.

Although only about 20% of the insured population in the area is enrolled in managed care, that number has grown over the past couple of years. Having committed to investigating the managed care organizations and sensing a potential threat to her practice, Cheryl begins exploring her options. In discussions with other psychologists at a professional association meeting, she learns that several have recently joined various health care organizations claiming to be IDSs.

She hears from some that they are seeking safety in numbers and that increased bargaining power comes from membership in an organization of some sort. However, each of the organizations seem to have both supporters and detractors. In particular, she hears "horror stories" of non-behavioral health professionals making clinical decisions about the appropriateness of a treatment plan, of care being denied arbitrarily, and of impossible demands for data by some of the organizations.

Cheryl decides to investigate each of the organizations and join only the best one.

2

Horizontal Integration

ALTHOUGH THERE is no ideal process for pursuing integration, perhaps the first step is joining with providers of like services, a strategy referred to as horizontal integration. However, before practitioners consider merging with or acquiring local and regional competitors, they must understand the issues associated with this strategy. This chapter addresses critical issues related to horizontal integration, including the basic concept, the rationale for pursuing this strategy, four common models, the process for achieving integration, and the caveats and potential pitfalls related to horizontal integration.

WHAT IS HORIZONTAL INTEGRATION?

Horizontal integration can be defined as a relationship among providers that offer similar or analogous services, as with a group of psychologists. Usually the relationship is based on sharing resources, infrastructure, and knowledge. To exemplify this concept, consider the following scenarios:

- Two computer manufacturers formed a horizontal coalition to procure microchips via a group purchasing arrangement, share laboratory space for research and development, and market their computers through the same channels or outlets.
- Another computer firm pursuing vertical integration purchased a microchip factory, engaged in the business of interconnectivity, produced and sold information technology peripherals, and started an after-market computer repair business.

As illustrated by these two scenarios, horizontal integration represents the association of firms that are in the same business, while vertical integration involves a combination of firms that are in complimentary businesses.

In behavioral health care, the most common form of horizontal integration has been the creation of multi-hospital systems or chains. Behavioral health professionals first experimented with integration more than 20 years ago by formulating horizontally integrated group practices. These enterprises were followed by first-generation managed care organizations such as preferred provider organizations (PPOs) and independent practice associations (IPAs), which were established primarily to attract payers by offering broad geographic coverage and discounted fees.

A second generation of horizontally integrated practitioner networks consists of group practices without walls (GPWWs) and management service organizations (MSOs) which have evolved not only to attract payers but also to reduce operating costs, amass the capital resources necessary to assume risk, develop name recognition in the market, and compete on the basis of differentiation. One recognizable but intangible benefit of horizontal integration has been how well such relationships have enabled practitioners to exchange knowledge and know how. Thus, horizontal integration is a strategy aimed at controlling administrative expenses and the costs of inconsistent capacity utilization while enhancing revenue and market share by offering payers the inherent advantages of a large, synergistic provider network.

WHY CONSIDER HORIZONTAL INTEGRATION?

Health care providers operate by principles that are unique in many ways. Not only must they make decisions that are consistent with their healing mission and professional ethics, they must also monitor the financial health of the organization to assure its continued survivability. In recent years, however, health care payers (including federal, state, and local governments, as well as employers and insurance companies) have played a significant role in reshaping health care delivery through reimbursement policy. While a provider may have a meritorious mission and vision, he or she must also respond to payer expectations in order to survive in a turbulent marketplace. Likewise, payers must respond to the needs of their customers (insured employees, transfer payment beneficiaries, and other individuals). This trickle down effect has compelled providers to offer comprehensive services through an improved delivery system, with all-inclusive access and at a lower cost per capita. These are the objectives of the marketplace and the very reasons practitioners may consider strategies such as horizontal integration as a means of achieving market-driven goals.

Although some form of managed care has been in existence since the 1970s, recent growth has been propelled by the payers' and employers' need to control costs while maintaining some level of benefits. Nationwide, managed care growth has been 10% per year with market penetration rates in excess of 50% in mature markets like the West Coast (over ninety million lives nationwide). Managed care market penetration can be thought of as the percentage of health care dollars that are paid to organizations providing services at a discount while coordinating care and managing utilization. High managed care market penetration statistics are red flags for providers. Historical analysis suggests that when the managed care penetration rate in a given market reaches 25%, mass consolidation of providers lies ahead. To be proactive, practitioners may want to begin seeking strategic partners when the managed care market reaches 10 to 15% penetration. Table 2 illustrates the typical market progression and approximate time frame for each phase.

Horizontal integration offers practitioners an opportunity to control

TABLE 2 Managed Care Market Progression

Characteristic	Now	1–2 Years	3–4 Years	5 Years
Payment mechanism	Fee-for-service	DRG/global pricing, discounts	Primary care capitation	Full risk
Common managed care organization (MCO)	PPO	IPA, HMO, POS, MSO	Group/network HMO	Integrated systems
Common mergers	Rural/affiliate network	Hospital-hospital MCO-MCO	Providers groups, horizontal integration	Vertical alignment
Continuum measures	PHO, home health	Sub-acute, LTC units; Post-acute channels	Pre-acute channels	Full continuum
HMO penetration	Less than 10%	10%–25%	25%–50%	Over 50%
Typical benchmark markets	Huntsville	Birmingham New Orleans	Atlanta Dallas	Southern California

quality, improve access, reduce costs, and monitor accountability on behalf of the managed care organization or payer. Payers are generally looking for a one-stop-shopping solution that provides a variety of practitioners and services. For example, payers prefer a single signature contract that provides plan members with crisis intervention, adolescent services, substance abuse treatment programs, psychological testing and other counseling services. Correspondingly, payers are concerned with the manner in which psychological services will be delivered. Networking allows practitioners to offer a more comprehensive health care product than solo-practitioners or isolated groups can offer.

Horizontal integration also enables practitioners to demand a voice in the quality and utilization management processes and treatment protocols required by the managed care plan. In order to satisfy the accreditation criteria for managed care plans, provider networks must be able to deliver convenient access to behavioral health care on a routine, urgent, and emergency basis with support staff available around the clock to deliver advice and manage triage. Likewise, standards must be met with regard to the number of offices open to accepting new members and the ratio of members to practitioners. The horizontally integrated networks will be expected to monitor:

- lead time necessary to schedule appointments
- acceptable driving times to practitioner offices
- maximum allowable queuing times once the patient arrives on location

In addition to the managed care contracting advantages, horizontal integration offers an opportunity to achieve economies of scale in administrative functions and shared infrastructure.

MODELS FOR HORIZONTAL INTEGRATION

To confront the challenges and garner the benefits mentioned above there are at least four alternative structures in practice today. While these structures should not be a substitute for creative thinking and customized relationships, they are models to consider. The first two models, PPOs and IPAs, are networks of otherwise independent practitioners who integrate in order to offer their services at a discounted fee-for-service or capitated rate to attract patients into their practices.

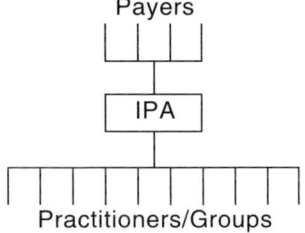

An IPA is an entity that assembles practitioners who will agree to provide services for discounted fees or assumes some form of financial risk. Because the practitioners delegate contracting authority to the IPA, the payer can sign a single contract and reap the benefits of geographic coverage, consistent quality, and predictable costs. The advantages from the practitioner's perspective are (a) access to managed care revenues, (b) increased patient volume and practice capacity utilization, (c) relative autonomy, and (d) administrative advantages such as

- information technology, including medical records and data processing, that facilitates tracking patient outcomes
- revenue enhancement, billing, accounts receivable, and cash management
- expense management, including employee benefits, payroll, and accounts payable functions
- group purchasing for supplies, services, and insurance
- financial, tax, and cost accounting
- human resource development, including professional recruiting and retention with direct connections to graduate programs and professional search firms
- marketing, public relations, and regional advertising
- legal services and contract negotiation
- resources including journals, periodicals, and videos
- peer support, periodic forums, and educational sessions
- a shared back office and technical staff with practice management expertise

Such improvements in economic efficiency coupled with increased patient loads can afford providers a healthier bottom line in spite of managed care discounts.

Horizontal integration will allow practitioners to join together to amass the resources necessary for developing an efficient infrastructure, establishing contracting clout with payers, and assuming risk under full capitation. Most importantly, these horizontal coalitions position networks to move toward vertical integration and eventually full integration while retaining substantial autonomy in comparison to payer-driven organizations.

It is important to point out that horizontal integration through an IPA has not proven to be a successful managed care strategy when the scope of services is narrowly defined. For example, forming a network of urologists may be appealing to the practitioners but not the purchasers of care because the only major benefit of the network is greater geographic coverage. Conversely, a coalition of behavioral health professionals can offer not only vast geographic coverage, but also a diverse scope of treatment programs. Managed care organizations frequently "carve out" behavioral health obligations and search for a network of psychologists, psychiatrists, and other behavioral health practitioners to provide comprehensive services to plan members.

PPO NETWORK

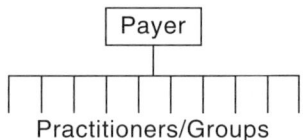

Practitioners/Groups

The PPO is a network of providers, generally created by payers wishing to control health care costs, in which payers contract with individual providers to deliver services at a discounted fee-for-service. Practitioners participating in PPOs often face a perplexing array of employer benefit plans with differing policies and procedures, including billing practices, reimbursement procedures, protocols, and utilization review procedures. Thus, a strong administrative infrastructure is necessary to keep abreast of the differing benefit plans. The main advantage to joining a PPO is that it enables providers to participate in managed care contracts while still maintaining a maximum degree of practice autonomy. However, these structures are not well suited to assuming risk, which limits their appeal to progressive health care organizations, employers, and payers.

While the intent of PPOs and IPAs is to obtain access to managed care revenue and maximize patient volume, the focus of an MSO is cost containment and practice support. An MSO is an organization that caters to practitioners by performing some or all of the administrative and prac-

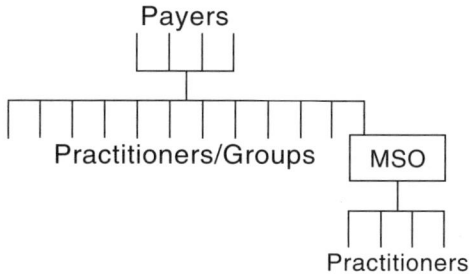

tice management functions that are not directly related to patient care, including practice management, computer support systems, accounting, purchasing, billing, and marketing. The average solo-practitioner, whether realizing it or not, devotes almost 20% of the work day to the non–revenue generating duties of practice management. Horizontal integration offers an opportunity to substantially reduce overhead costs and increase practice income by redirecting this time to direct patient care and productive services.

MSOs may take several legal forms but are typically organized as a corporation with single or joint ownership among participating practitioners and health care institutions. In some MSOs, non-owner practitioners are permitted to participate by purchasing services. In an MSO, practitioners retain their individual revenue streams and are responsible for managing their own individual office environments. In a few instances, MSOs have been successful contracting vehicles. However, some states require MSOs that accept capitation to register as an HMO with the Department of Insurance. Additionally, antitrust laws and other regulatory impediments may prevent MSO participants from engaging in collective contract negotiations. As with any strategic alternative, the legal implications must be fully assessed. Overall, the MSO allows practitioners to maintain their practice style, geographic location, and autonomy while enjoying the benefits of centralized administrative management and support infrastructure.

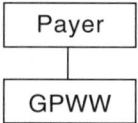

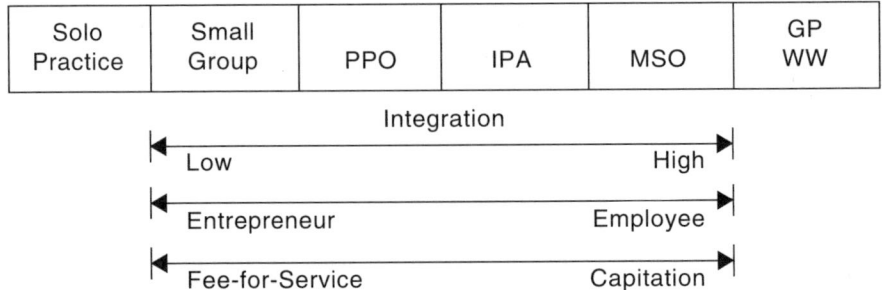

FIGURE 1   Comparison of models' economic and operational integration.

Though the models described above address specific elements of the managed care philosophy, the fourth model represents the epitome of flexible horizontal integration structures. The GPWW strategy requires a great deal of commitment by the practitioner, but the rewards include increased income, cost containment, sustained growth, and practice/lifesytle balance. In a GPWW, the practitioner sells his assets to a newly formed professional corporation or partnership. However, the practitioner maintains his geographic location and practices as an employee of and shareholder in the new organization. The previously independent practices become unincorporated divisions of the newly formed organization.

Along with maintaining the existing office, the practitioner may enjoy autonomy with respect to scheduling, policy and procedure development, human resource selection, and practice style. However, revenue from fees and capitation contracts are owned by the new organization. Compensation takes many forms, including salaries, bonuses, and profit sharing. Global policy making is vested in the new board of directors or other governing body, depending on the legal structure. One rationale behind economically integrating the practices is to comply with the morass of antitrust, fee splitting, "fraud and abuse," and self-referral prohibitions (discussed in Chapter 5).

As illustrated in Figure 1, this model represents a much higher level of economic and operational integration than with an IPA, PPO, or MSO. However, this structure is best positioned for accepting capitated revenue streams and long-term success.

THE PROCESS OF HORIZONTAL INTEGRATION

Integration strategies are developed, evaluated, and selected via the strategic planning process, which is discussed in greater detail in the APA

Practitioner's Toolbox Series volume *Building a Group Practice: Creating a Shared Vision for Success*. The first phase in the strategic planning process involves determining practitioner goals and customer needs. The provider begins by defining the group's vision, mission, objectives, expectations, and measurable goals. For example, that vision may be to establish a superior integrated system of care that can be used as a model for behavioral health care organizations throughout the country. The mission statement specifically defines the target market, service scope, geographic coverage, strategic alliances, and level of commitment to the community and indigent patient populations. Objectives, expectations, and goals are narrowly defined, measurable, and have realistic time frames. For instance, the organization may strive to establish a premier quality provider network throughout an entire metropolitan statistical area within 5 years while cutting administrative costs by 15%.

Practitioner vision, mission, and goals should be formulated around customer needs and desires. Thus, target market and service offerings are a function of the behavioral health care needs of the population and the current supply and level of quality of existing providers. Specifically, one community may have a need for geriatric day treatment services, while another may need an evening chemical dependency treatment program for young adults. The provider identifies behavioral health care needs and positions the practice to serve unmet needs.

Once community needs have been determined, the provider may want to consider payer requirements and any external factors that may impede strategic alternatives. External factors include income levels, legal issues, regulatory requirements, political agendas, capital requirements, and competitor strengths. For instance, a community may need an eating disorder treatment program; however, if the services cannot be funded, the need may go unmet. The provider may assess the feasibility of offering this service with regards to payers' reimbursement methodologies and program criteria. If program revenue is generated from self-paying patients, the provider may also want to assess income levels in the target market.

Overall, the provider first defines his or her desires and direction, assesses customer needs, and then evaluates any barriers to entry before searching for a partner. It is important to note the entire vision, mission, and goal development process must be revisited throughout the partner evaluation and selection process.

Understanding an individual practitioner's or group's existing strengths and weaknesses is also a critical part of the initial phase. Current practice characteristics such as geographic location, financial condition, market share, community perception, information technology, and practice management infrastructure may be evaluated or assessed. These characteristics may be categorized as either strengths or weaknesses depending upon one's point of view. As described below, this exercise may help to identify which characteristics to market and look for when selecting a strategic partner.

The second phase, searching for a partner or partners, begins by developing a set of criteria for use in identifying and evaluating prospective partners. This checklist may include a similar mission, complimentary services, strategic location, and favorable image. Once partners have been identified, the parties move forward by establishing guiding principles for the organization (i.e., revisit the vision, mission, objectives, and goals). This process is participatory from the onset and includes all of the key decision makers in the organization.

Next, the practitioners discuss and formulate possible integration structures, keeping in mind that the underlying goal is to establish a relationship that is mutually beneficial and does not require molding two entities into a boiler-plate organizational structure. Once it appears as though the structure meets the needs of the participants, the legal and economic implications of the proposed alternative may be assessed with counsel, including legal and financial expertise. Assessing contribution to the bottom line may be one factor in the evaluation, along with vision, mission, objective, and goals of the coalition as illustrated in the partner assessment matrix that follows. For optimal results, a potential partner will complement the strengths and weaknesses of the other practitioners (like Partners A and D in Figure 2). Combining two practices with the same weaknesses may not be advisable. Obviously, Partner B would appear to be an ideal candidate partner for any practice.

Developing a business plan with financial statements for at least three years enables the two organizations to make hard business and clinical service line decisions and formulate assumptions about service offerings, organizational structure, capital investments, compensation, and equity distribution. Since this process can be expensive and time consuming, it is often performed concurrently with the due diligence review. Due diligence is the process of scrutinizing the clinical, practice management, financial, and legal aspects of the organization. An all-encompassing confirmation process, due diligence includes a review of the information outlined in Table 3.

If practices are being bought or sold, practice valuations by an experienced, objective professional mutually agreed upon by the involved parties may help to avoid conflict.

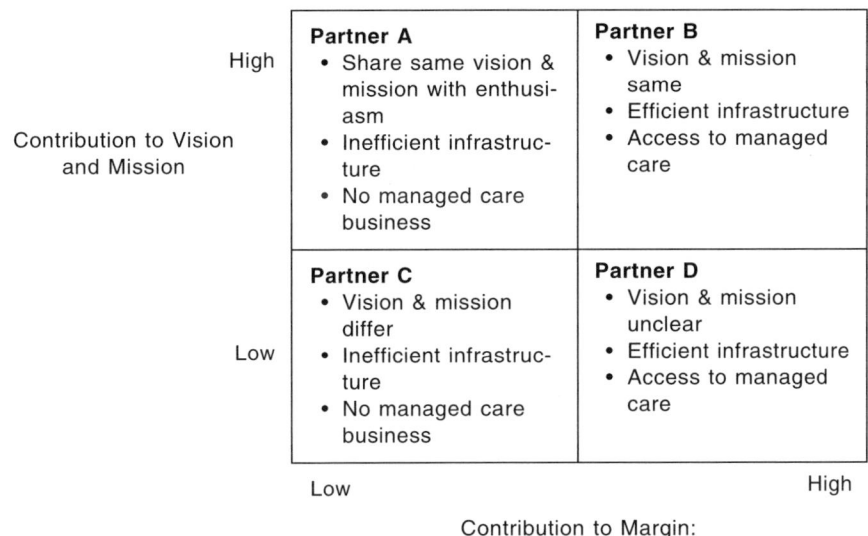

FIGURE 2   Partner assessment matrix.

Phase 3

The final phase in the integration process is selecting a partner, finalizing the structure, and implementing the strategy. However, as with any important matter, the strategy is continually evaluated for effectiveness and modified as necessary to meet changing conditions.

SOME CAVEATS TO HORIZONTAL INTEGRATION

Working closely with a former competitor is not always easy. Like any other relationship, a horizontal coalition has its downside. In theory, individual practitioners that perform the same or very similar activities can combine like functions to achieve economies of scale. However, in reality, practice styles, values, politics, and cultures may differ enough to block coalitions or neutralize their benefits. A practitioner's personal agenda may supersede organizational objectives and nullify the advantages of integration. Likewise, when it comes to merging finances, compensation disagreements may arise. For many providers, economic survival is the primary driver behind integration. However, the costs of integration in

TABLE 3 Information Analyzed in Due Diligence Review

Clinical	Practice Management	Financial	Legal and Contractual
• Practitioner credentialing/licensure information • Audit of sample medical charts • Documentation of pending and historical claims • Malpractice/medical-legal claims • Program descriptions, participation, outcomes • Patient origin • Referral network activity	• Organization chart • Policies and procedures • Employee manual • Employee compensation and benefits information • Payer mix • Procedure/treatment plan—productivity report (e.g., visits per practitioner per day) • Procedure/treatment plan—coding report with associated charges (e.g., top 10 diagnoses)	• 3 years financial report • Tax returns • Program revenue detail • Managed care payment and bonus reports • Payroll and bonus schedules • Benefits plans • Insurance policies • Leases depreciation and amortization schedules • Insurance policies	• Articles of incorporation • Partnership and shareholder agreements • Employment agreements • Managed care agreements • Other contractual agreements

terms of personal preferences and tolerances are also important when assessing the choices in relationships.

SUMMARY

Horizontal integration is a first step toward an integrated delivery system. It is particularly important because the non-hospital based provider can achieve increased power in negotiating with payers and that power affects not only financial results but quality of care issues such as access, backup, and peer support.

CASE STUDY

Cheryl Logan, PhD, has discovered from her discussions with other practitioners that three basic types of organizations exist in her community: PHOs and MSOs created by several local hospitals and an IPA started by some physicians. She has previously met the director of one MSO, so she calls him up to discuss the organization in greater detail.

She is surprised to learn she is already a member of the MSO by virtue of being on staff at the sponsoring hospital. However, since her office staff handles all of her administrative needs, she has not been "taking advantage of the benefits of the membership." She learns that, for a small fee, the MSO will convert her paper bills into an electronic data file and submit it to payers so that she can collect from them more quickly. She also learns that the MSO offers a free membership to a discount warehouse for office equipment and supplies and that it delivers weekly at no charge. The MSO has several purchasing contracts to pass along substantial discounts on services ranging from legal counsel to janitorial services. Finally, she learns that the MSO runs a personnel agency to recruit and train office staff as well as replace missing staff on a temporary basis. However, it does not get involved in contracting with payers. The director says "our mission is to help our members control their administrative costs and reduce business hassles." He suggests, however, that the other MSO in town does contract for its members.

When Cheryl meets with the director of the other MSO, she is surprised at the differences. This MSO performs all accounting functions for its membership, negotiates discounts and contracts with payers on their behalf, and owns the office buildings where its members practice. In fact, the office staff at each practice are employees, not of the practice, but of the MSO. The MSO contracts with several payers on a discounted fee-for-service basis. The MSO is developing plans to apply for a license as an HMO in the next year so that it can contract on a capitated rate basis directly with local employers. The director explains that they "have not yet gotten into behavioral health services since it is such a small portion of the health care dollars." But he also expresses an interest in working with Cheryl to develop a network of behavioral health providers as part of the HMO's product line.

Later, as she talks with the IPA director, Cheryl hears about its plans to monitor quality using claims data with quarterly "report cards" issued to the members and perhaps the public. She tours the IPA's utilization review department, where nurses "certify" admissions and treatment plans, and meets the IPA's medical director, a retired pathologist, who explains that the IPA relies upon a quality improvement (QI) committee and peer review process to evaluate clinical efficiency and effectiveness. When asked about behavioral health care needs, the medical director explains that a locally recognized psychiatrist consults with the QI committee but is not a voting member. He explains that, as allied health professionals, "psychologists are not eligible for membership in the IPA but can contract to provide care."

Armed with marketing materials, application forms, and bylaws from each organization, Cheryl develops a decision matrix to evaluate how each would help her practice prosper. The MSO she already belongs to offers a lot of worthwhile services she can take advantage of to reduce costs.

However, membership in it will not address the loss of referrals to managed care organizations. The second MSO's approach would result in a significant loss of practice autonomy. Particularly, the idea of someone else deciding who to hire or fire as her receptionist is unacceptable. The IPA's attitude toward behavioral health care leaves much to be desired. She is especially uncomfortable with the idea of peer review by medical physicians with no specialized training in behavioral health. She resolves to keep looking for an organization that will meet her needs.

3

Vertical Integration

THE GOAL FOR VERTICAL *integration is control over the continuum of care to achieve a cost advantage over competitors in the market. Vertical integration most often begins with hospital expansion into post-acute services such as day treatment. Later, the hospital may seek to "partner" with providers to solidify its referral channels.*

This chapter examines vertical integration as a market strategy, typical forms of vertical integration, including PHOs, relevant models for behavioral health care providers, and advantages and disadvantages of vertical integration.

VERTICAL INTEGRATION

In the simplest terms, a vertically integrated delivery system is one in which all necessary levels and types of care are available. If specialized services are not routinely offered by a member of the system, they are nonetheless available through a contractual agreement with a non-member. A system is not fully integrated if any patient need is permitted to "fall through the cracks" or requires an ad-hoc agreement to be negotiated. To encourage efficiency in the delivery of care, all levels of care are be integrated into a single organization of some type that receives payment on behalf of all components of the delivery system and distributes the revenue according to some methodology other than fee-for-service. Many vertically integrated systems rely upon a budget process, others purchase services using capitation rates, and still others own the components and employ the caregivers.

To measure efficiency, most vertically integrated systems rely upon care management processes such as protocols designed by multi-disciplin-

TABLE 4   Continuum Chart

Fee-for-Service Indemnity Market	Managed/Discounted Indemnity Market	Capitated/At-Risk Managed Market
Basic care, including: • Acute care • Residential treatment centers (RTCs) • Outpatient programs • Employee assistance programs	Add: • Partial hospitalization • Day treatment • Crisis intervention • Evening programs	Add: • Telephone triage • Halfway houses • Community centers • Hospital-based crisis/stabilization centers • Intensive outpatient • Home health care • School counseling centers • Other, as necessary

ary teams and retrospective analysis of practice pattern statistics to reinforce desired treatment behaviors and punish offenders. One of the most basic behaviors monitored is utilization of the continuum of services to reduce costs.

In behavioral health, the continuum of care may be an extremely complex mix of public, private, and charitable organizations. One advantage of this increased continuum is the delivery of treatment in less restrictive environments and with, at least potentially, less stigma. Table 4 outlines many of the component services in a vertically integrated behavioral health system and the phase at which they are commonly added to the system's continuum.

For example, combining a half-way house with outpatient programs may create an effective and more appropriate alternative to a Residential Treatment Center (RTC).

MARKET STRATEGY

A delivery system in which referrals are made to less expensive providers whenever possible has a substantial cost advantage over a system where providers do not cooperate with each other to provide care in the most appropriate setting. The underlying assumption is that relative costs of different modalities are known to all providers of care within the system and outcomes are generally equivalent across the continuum. Assumptions regarding costs and outcome need to be continually validated. Therefore, a vertically integrated delivery system will develop mechanisms and systems for accurately determining the costs and outcomes of care in order to gain and sustain its cost advantage over competitors.

False economies may be achieved by reducing costs without regard to outcomes. Readmissions and recidivism are especially critical in behavioral health care. An inexpensive treatment modality that frequently fails its clients will not produce cost savings for the delivery system over the long term.

While an ideal system for monitoring outcomes across a continuum of providers may not exist today, systems do exist to measure readmissions, recidivism, lost work days, days free of abused substance, and other indicators that can be collected and analyzed in conjunction with financial data. This analysis is typically performed by the integrated delivery system, but some functions, especially data collection, may be delegated to individual providers of care.

It will be necessary for practitioners to agree to meet cost control expectations and reorient their practices if necessary. The goal is to avoid providing any care that does not give incremental benefit to the member/patient/client. The practitioner is expected to maximize benefit at minimal cost. Figure 3 illustrates this concept.

Many of the vertically integrated delivery systems began with hospital expansion efforts aimed at survival. Over the past decade, hospitals have

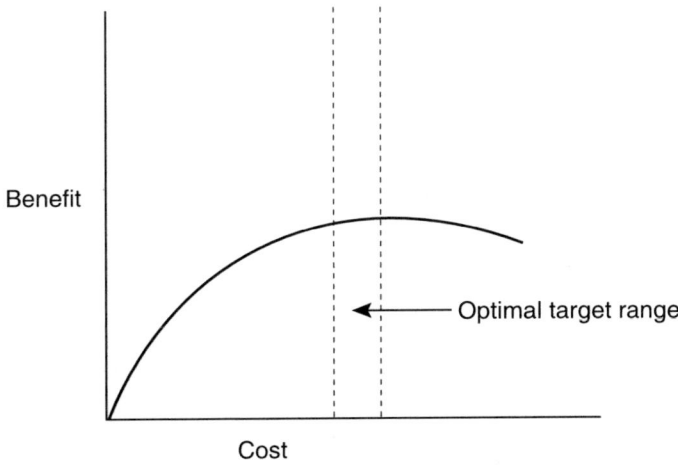

FIGURE 3   Cost–benefit tradeoff of care.

seen a substantial decline in the inpatient census, partially because of improvements in technology that have supported a shift to ambulatory care, but also driven by Medicare payment reforms and increased utilization monitoring by payers. Seeking to sustain their organizations, many hospitals expanded their services into non-acute care, including ambulatory treatment via partial hospitalization, day programs, and outpatient sessions. With these programs, hospitals can shift some fixed and overhead costs as well as staff from the acute setting to generate revenue, reduce losses, and remain solvent and relevant. Under increasing pressure from payers, some hospitals have created behavioral home health services, on-campus half-way houses, and other innovative services designed to expand the continuum of care toward less costly alternatives to inpatient care.

Recently, some hospitals have begun to "reach-out" to their providers in an effort to increase their loyalty in terms of referrals, bind them contractually, or recognize their importance as referral sources. Although some of these efforts have been subject to scrutiny from the federal government for antitrust and self-referral issues, others reflect good business sense. Some hospitals have chosen to fund the start-up of MSOs to assist their provider staffs with group purchasing, computer support, billing services, and other administrative practice support as a means of "rewarding" their loyalty. Although helpful in reducing the administrative overhead expenses of a practice, MSOs may not be good vehicles for managed care contracting because of the antitrust concerns that may arise when practices are not financially integrated. As discussed in chapter 5, practices that do not share risk, as in an MSO, are generally prohibited from collaborating to set prices.

By contrast, formation of a vertically integrated delivery system permits hospitals and providers to work together legally in the pursuit of mutually beneficial solutions to market challenges. By definition, a PHO is a joint venture between hospital(s) and practitioners to integrate the continuum of care. The PHO contracts with payers on behalf of the partners and assumes some responsibility for credentialing, utilization management, customer service, or other value-added duties. Payers and MCOs prefer the one-signature contract, which delivers an established network.

If initiated by a hospital, control of the PHO's management may be vested with the hospital. When initiated by a horizontally integrated group of practitioners, like an IPA, management control is more likely to be vested with the practitioners. The issue of management control is critical for two reasons:

Financial Management

The allocation of revenues and risk sharing is subject to negotiation but will ultimately be determined by the body in control of the PHO (whether that is the hospital or the IPA).

Clinical Management

Balancing access, utilization, quality, and outcomes requires an investment in systems, procedures, personnel, and protocols. The nature of these control and measurement processes will be determined by the body in control of the PHO.

As the nature of health care changes and bed days decline, the hospital's role and importance declines. Several IPAs, for example, in Southern California have negotiated large managed care contracts that permit them latitude in buying hospital services as "commodities." In other words, no hospital is a primary party to the contract.

Paul M. Ellwood, MD, of the Jackson Hole Group, pioneered the concept of the PHO in the early 1980s. Hospitals have come to consider PHOs one strategy for ensuring their survival under managed care. To the extent that PHOs can coordinate care to improve outcomes while reducing costs, this strategy may prove worthwhile. However, the issue of management control is critical in a practitioner's consideration of this integration option.

PHO MODELS

Three distinct models and one hybrid PHO model exist depending largely upon whether the hospital initiated the vertical integration or the practitioners integrated horizontally first. The hospital-initiated PHO most commonly follows an open model in which each member of the hospital's staff is encouraged to participate in the PHO. Each practitioner is an independent contractor to the PHO, as shown in Figure 4.

Of the approximately 2,000 PHOs in America, 90% are open models. One of the primary advantages of the open model is that the hospital avoids ostracizing any practitioners in this process. The obvious disadvantage is that when providers are not selected on the basis of performance criteria, utilization controls are unlikely to produce sufficient savings to attract payers.

If, on the other hand, an IPA or other practitioner-directed entity

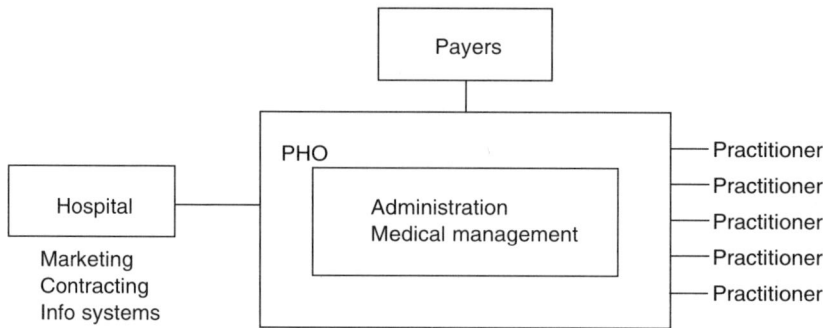

FIGURE 4 Open model PHO initiated by hospital.

initiates the PHO, the model is more likely to achieve substantial cost reductions and resemble Figure 5.

Both open models are likely to exist as interim organizations designed to permit trust building and managed care expertise. Over time, they may evolve into closed model PHOs, which often feature increased capitation contracting, clinical protocols and credentialing of practitioners based upon outcomes, efficiency, and effectiveness. Although the organizational structure of a closed model PHO is the same as that of an open model, practitioner membership is restrictive. As a result, the members are more likely to be a highly cohesive group with similar practice values and standards of care.

Additionally, a closed PHO routinely restricts membership by specialists to specific targets based upon membership need estimates.

Another model, a pluralistic or multi-level PHO, may be considered

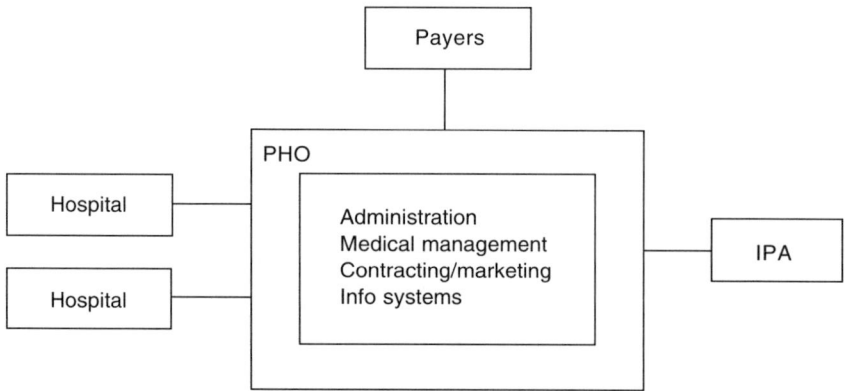

FIGURE 5 Practitioner driven PHO.

the transitional organization between the open and closed PHO. Although all practitioners can become members of the PHO, only selected practitioners are permitted to join certain sub-panels, which are paid on a capitated basis as in Figure 6.

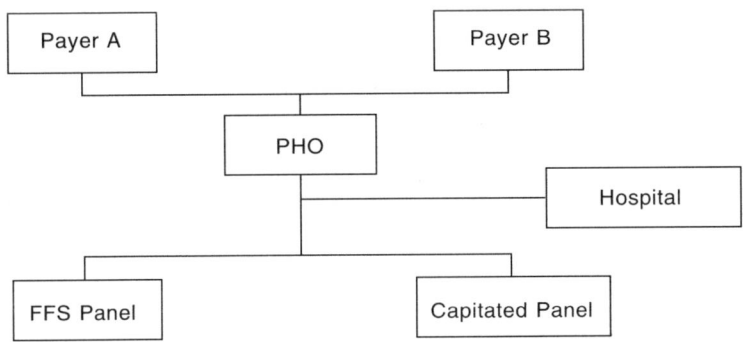

FIGURE 6   Pluralistic PHO.

This sub-panel approach permits the PHO to gain experience with risk sharing arrangements while continuing with its discounted fee-for-service agreements. One additional use of the multi-level PHO is Medicaid contracting when not all PHO practitioners wish to serve Medicaid recipients.

PHO GOVERNANCE

As outlined above, management control is an important factor in PHO development. Practitioner initiation of the PHO may no longer be an option in some markets, where a large number of PHOs have already been formed. In this case, a careful examination of the PHO's organizational documents is appropriate. Among the considerations are:

Governance participation

Practitioner representation and voting rights on the board are important. Even if the hospital has less than 50% of the board seats, the voting process may result in veto power for the hospital. Additionally, the mechanism for selecting board members and the rotation schedule for selecting members may give advantages to the hospital.

Reserved powers

The hospital may retain special authority or powers. One common example is credentialing. Some PHOs require that all practitioners maintain active admitting privileges at the hospital to be a member of the PHO. In essence, practitioners who do not admit are disempowered and have no voice in governance.

Management Appointments

The hospital may seek to retain authority over hiring and firing of PHO administrative staff. How well the PHO's board can manage may be impaired by this issue.

Committee Appointments

Practitioners should definitely control appointments to all medical management committees, including quality management, utilization control, credentialing, and protocol development. Practitioners should have representation on all other committees. The hospital should not have approval authority over committee appointments.

In summary, some hospitals seek to form PHOs for survival reasons and see them as mere extensions of hospital operations. Over the long term, a more equitable arrangement that shares power as well as risk is preferable.

CLINICAL MANAGEMENT

Most PHOs are now preparing for accreditation requirements, either independently or in cooperation with an MCO that has delegated some management responsibilities to the PHO. Both accreditation agencies require the network to implement extensive processes for measuring, comparing, and improving the quality of service and care. Two accreditation agencies currently exist:

- *Joint Commission for Accreditation of Healthcare Organizations* (JCAHO), based in Chicago, uses a survey process very similar to that used for hospitals and accommodates a variety of networks.
- *National Committee for Quality Assurance* (NCQA), a relatively

new organization, based in Washington, DC, was created by a coalition of large employers specifically to accredit MCOs. NCQA has also created the Health Plan Employer Data Information Set (HEDIS), a performance comparison process thath includes some indicators for behavioral health services. NCQA appears to be becoming an industry standard for evaluating HMOs.

NCQA emphasizes protocol development and comprehensive health management, while JCAHO relies upon more traditional systems and episodes of care for clinical management purposes. In general, if payment is not capitated, the following utilization control mechanisms may be expected from any PHO:

- pre-admission certification
- concurrent review (daily concurrent review or target length of stay system)
- pre-procedure review for ambulatory services
- second opinion on selected procedures (e.g., ECT)
- fourth generation utilization review

Under capitation, the need for an intrusive utilization control process is diminished; however, some PHOs continue the process.

Most PHOs also utilize case or care management for high cost or high risk cases including trauma, HIV infection, and inpatient behavioral health care. Typically, the case manager functions as a member/patient liaison to help guide the patient through the continuum of care and reduce the readmission/recidivism rate. Working under the guidance of the provider, the care manager may function as a discharge planner, social worker, or telephone triage nurse to permit intervention at a lower level of care than would be necessary if the situation went unidentified. Care managers usually follow their assigned cases for lengthy periods and may develop a "sixth sense" about their assignments. Care managers may also make home visits, functioning as a provider-extender.

Care managers also participate in developing protocols, which are standardized treatment plans for an "idealized" normal course of a specific condition. Protocols for behavioral health conditions should be developed in cooperation with a multidisciplinary team of practitioners and circulated for review and input before implementation. Protocol development by a committee of the PHO or other group that does not include appropriate representation is problematic. Additional information and discussion of clinical management processes is available in the APA Practitioner's Toolbox Series volume *Building a Group Practice: Creating a Shared Vision for Success.*

Performance measurement is a routine function for a PHO. However, behavioral health practitioners should have input into the selection of indicators for profiling and designation of peers for comparison purposes. Common indicators include:

- average length of inpatient stay
- ratio of partial days to inpatient days
- readmission rate
- compliance with protocol rate
- adverse occurrences (e.g., suicide, overdose)
- escalation rate (moves backwards along the continuum to a higher level of care)
- avoidable inpatient days
- customer satisfaction rating
- days/1000, admissions/1000 (common standards of system performance)

Most common profiling systems display individual performance compared to the prior period (quarter or year) and to the peer average. Some systems show the percentile achieved by the individual in comparison to the peer group. With such feedback, some practitioners modify their practice patterns to more closely resemble the peer norms resulting in cost containment. To support and encourage such alteration in behavior, some PHOs develop descriptions of "best practices" for each profile indicator, pinpointing variances that may be causative. For example, a lower readmission rate may be seen among practitioners whose patients are routinely followed for more than two weeks after discharge by a home health agency social worker. The profile is a critical component of credentialing as the PHO prepares to assume risk. As illustrated in Table 5, the PHO's credentialing process becomes increasingly restrictive as the PHO shifts from an Open Model to a Closed Model in preparation for risk contracting.

SUMMARY

Vertical integration may begin with formation of a PHO that evolves into an effective continuum of care and a substantial cost advantage over

TABLE 5 PHO Shift From an Open to Closed Model

Open	Multi-Level	Closed
• Valid license • National databank clearance • Minimum liability insurance • Medical staff member	Add: • Board certification • Cost efficient • Acceptable outcomes • Client/patient satisfaction	Add: • Specialty need • Value oriented • Good profile

other networks. To achieve this evolution, the PHO will implement clinical management processes and performance profiling systems.

Case Study

Cheryl Logan's attempts to set up meetings with the two PHOs in her community reveal that one is an open model PHO developed by a hospital where she maintains privileges and one is a closed model. The first welcomes her interest and supplies her with a provider manual as well as marketing materials and a membership application. The other PHO informs her that its capitated panel of behavioral health providers is presently full but they agree to mail her a provider packet so she could apply for a position on the referral panel that takes "overflow" patients.

Cheryl reviews the materials from the open model PHO and finds the fee schedule is very low, the utilization review protocols are very intrusive with prior authorization required every four visits, and physical health practitioners make decisions about behavioral health needs.

The material from the other PHO reveals it is a pluralistic model with provider subpanels. In order to join the capitated provider panel, she must submit documentation of treatment outcomes, results of a patient satisfaction survey, and an analysis of her cost effectiveness compared to her peers as well as her credentials. After a 1-year appointment to the PHO's referral panel, the PHO will evaluate her profile to determine whether to admit her to the capitated panel, retain her in the referral panel, or terminate her participation.

Again, Cheryl finds out that none of the organizations fulfill her needs.

4

Fully Integrated Delivery Systems

FULLY INTEGRATED *delivery systems are expected to achieve market dominance over other networks during the next decade because of their ability to meet market demands as well as their cost advantages. This chapter examines three models for fully integrated delivery systems as well as the strengths and weaknesses of each model from both the payer and practitioner point of view.*

MARKET DOMINANCE

Fully integrated delivery systems offer payers a substantially improved contracting option over other networks because they combine the best features of horizontally integrated networks with the full continuum of care available from a PHO. A fully integrated delivery system (FIDS) is one organization that can meet all patient treatment needs without referral to non-network sources. Further, a fully integrated delivery system is one in which all provider incentives have been examined and theoretically aligned to reward appropriate, cost effective care. From a patient's point of view, a delivery system is fully integrated when demographic and clinical information are confirmed at each encounter instead of being redundantly collected.

In general, organizations that have achieved full integration have developed the administrative and clinical efficiencies to achieve a significant cost advantage over other networks as well as the resources and infrastructure to support capitated contracting and full assumption of risk. Table 6 summarizes key payer expectations and the corresponding characteristics commonly found in a FIDS.

TABLE 6 Payer Expectations and Features of IDSs

Payer Demands	IDS Features
One-stop-shopping	Vertical and horizontal integration • Continuum of care • Single contracting authority • Geographic access
Low cost	Shared infrastructure • Low administrative expenses (after start-up)
	Treatment guidelines • Use of continuum • Best practices
	Cost advantage (20% below other networks)
Risk assumption	Capitation is preferred payment mechanism • Aligned incentives • Cash flow

Payers are demanding one-stop-shopping, so providers are joining together to authorize contracts through a single signature. Payers also are demanding lowering overall costs, so providers are reducing their administrative staffs and sharing resources. Payers are demanding that providers accept risk so providers are forming organizations that can bear risk.

The importance of a 20% cost advantage cannot be overstated. In essence, if the IDS contracts at the market's average premium, it will achieve a 20% profit margin on the account. More importantly, the IDS can cut its premium for prestigious target accounts, which will influence decision making on other accounts. Alternatively, the IDS has the option to play a cost leadership strategy designed to drive out market competitors.

One of the less commonly considered advantages an IDS has in the market is the ability to attract and retain the talented practitioners necessary to deliver quality care at substantially reduced costs. Obviously, if the IDS experienced high turnover at key clinical positions, its reputation in the market would decline with a corresponding loss of contracts and members. Additionally, treatment guidelines and outcomes measurement would be sacrificed if practitioner turnover was commonplace. Loyalty of clinicians to the network is critical in aligning incentives and controlling costs. Table 7 summarizes the key elements of developing this competitive edge in the market place.

For example, when recruiting a practitioner, the IDS can offer to renovate and furnish office space, purchase computer systems, and other subsi-

TABLE 7   The Competitive Edge with Providers

Other Networks	IDS
• Mixed incentives for practitioner (fee-for-service) patients are 70% or more of practice volume • Subsidies illegal • Practitioner plans for retirement	• Single incentive system (profit sharing) for all payment sources • Subsidies common for office renovation, infrastructure needs • Practitioner can "cash out" at retirement

dies that are considered private inurement if offered by a less integrated network. In particular, federal regulations prohibit such compensation if it appears to be in return for referrals or admissions.

IDS MODELS

Fully integrated delivery systems come in three distinct models. As shown in the following charts, the staff model is probably the best known, but the foundation model and the equity model offer certain advantages to the practitioner. All three models have substantially improved survival chances over the less integrated networks described in previous chapters.

Staff Model

The staff model (see Figure 7) is ideally suited to assume financial risk as an organization. Practitioners are employees of the IDS which performs all administrative functions and duties.

Some practitioners value the lifestyle offered by this model, including shorter hours, less call, paid vacations, and educational opportunities, plus freedom to concentrate on treatment instead of marketing. In states where it is legal for a corporation to employ practitioners, a staff model may be

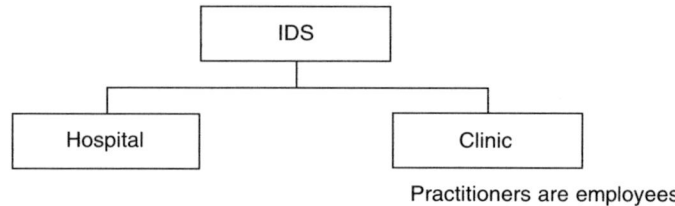

FIGURE 7   Staff model.

TABLE 8 Strengths and Weaknesses of Staff Model

Strengths	Weaknesses
• Stable practitioner income with benefits • Well known model • Predictable practice demands • Safe harbor from legal constraints • Predictable lifestyle/hours • No capital required to start or buy into a practice	• High capital costs • High legal costs • Loss of some clinical autonomy • Potentially less service oriented • Reputation

the ideal. Legal costs and other up-front costs are high, but maintenance costs are low. See Table 8 for a summary of this model's strengths and weaknesses.

Foundation Model

The foundation (see Figure 8) is an organization that owns and manages all practices in the network. The foundation contracts directly with payers, often on an exclusive basis. Most often, it is a non-profit, tax-exempt organization and employs all staff permitted under state law. The foundation owns, operates, and manages all practice sites, medical records, computer systems, and other equipment. The foundation receives payment, not on behalf of the practitioner, but as the provider of care. Practitioners are paid incentive bonuses and salaries in addition to profit or revenue-sharing plans.

In states that prohibit direct employment of clinicians by corporations, the foundation model is the best available for full integration.

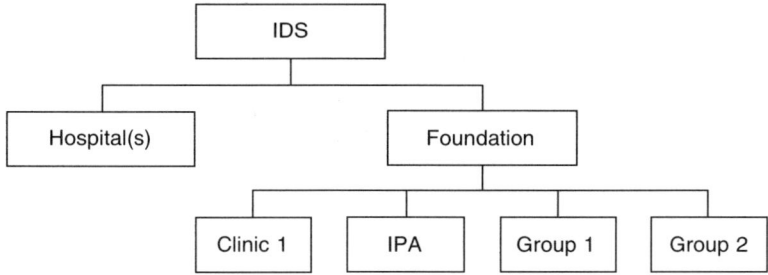

FIGURE 8 Foundation model.

TABLE 9   Strengths and Weaknesses of Foundation Model

Strengths	Weaknesses
• Tax avoidance (income and property) • Stable practitioner income with up-side incentives • Reputation/market perception (non-profit) • Negotiating clout with hospitals • Practitioner directed and dominated	• Loss of autonomy • Legally complex • High capital costs

The foundation model is especially appealing because of its practitioner orientation. For example, growth of a large IPA into a foundation requires partnering with a hospital organization to fund capital costs and conversion of all staff to foundation employees. See Table 9 for a summary of the strengths and weakneses of the foundation model.

Equity Model

The equity model IDS (see Figure 9) is owned and governed by practitioners—a twist on the staff model in which the practitioners not only receive a salary and bonuses but become shareholders in the IDS in lieu of immediate cash payments for their practices. Because practitioners own equity, they may be more supportive of medical management processes for controlling costs of care.

The equity model IDS has the option of purchasing a hospital, which would give the organization direct control over the costs of inpatient care but would require capital, or contracting for hospital services on a commodity basis like any other supply item. See Table 10 for a summary of this model's strengths and weaknesses.

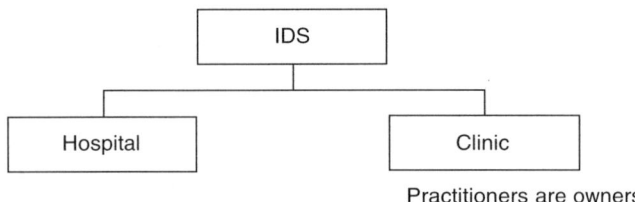

FIGURE 9   Equity model.

TABLE 10 Strengths and Weaknesses of Equity Model

Strengths	Weaknesses
• For-profit motive (taxable) • Practitioner controlled • Align incentives even more closely • Maintains entrepreneurial spirit • Low turnover • Low capital requirements • Legal safe harbor • Fast growth opportunity • Supports practitioner retirement planning	• Unfamiliar model • Limited capital for investment

SUMMARY

Because of their cost advantages and sensitivity to market demands, IDSs are expected to achieve market dominance over the next decade. Foundation, equity, and staff models offer distinct advantages and disadvantages that may influence the practitioner's decision regarding alliance.

CASE STUDY

Cheryl and three other practitioners outline the characteristics of an ideal delivery system over dinner. Their outline, centering on the individual provider's authority to make therapeutic decisions affecting the patient, is summarized below:

- Providers are empowered to provide care without interference from utilization review nurses.
- The primary care provider is not a gatekeeper for behavioral health needs.
- Practitioners share in the rewards that result from improvements in efficiency and effectiveness of care.
- The organization assists the practitioner with office support but does not dictate processes.
- Practice autonomy is a basic value.
- The organization is simple, legal, and provider-driven.

All four practitioners agree that a staff model and a foundation will not meet these desired characteristics and resolve to pursue the concept of an equity model system. One practitioner, Jim Moncrief, plans to meet with an attorney to ensure that collaborating does not raise legal issues. Mike Byrd agrees to research capital funding sources while his partner, Carla Linden, investigates organizational structure issues.

PART II

How to Build an Integrated Delivery System

5

Achieving Integration

INTEGRATION IS NEVER EASY. *Working collaboratively with former competitors and with other provider organizations is difficult. This chapter shifts the focus from "what" and "why" to "how." Legal and tax issues are outlined in this chapter to assist with network development. To achieve integration, agreement must be developed on the legal structure, tax status, governance, scope of services to be included, degree of financial risk assumed, and administrative structure for the network. One important consideration for the newly evolving network is the impact of antitrust laws on health care mergers and provider integration. Once an understanding of the federal rules affecting networks has been achieved, appropriate decisions can be made to avoid the threat of legal action. Naturally, this document cannot substitute for competent legal counsel with expertise in health care as well as state legislation potentially affecting negotiations.*

FEDERAL SCRUTINY OF PROVIDERS

Antitrust issues settled in courts regarding IDSs have relied most heavily on the answers to the following questions:

1. What is the degree of integration?
2. What is the market power of the venture?
3. Does the arrangement significantly foreclose development of competing groups?
4. Does the implemented contract unduly restrict competition within or outside the venture?

Whenever providers who have been competitors enter into an agreement, particularly in sensitive areas like the joint negotiation of price or the exclusion of other providers, antitrust issues may arise. Thus antitrust issues almost always need to be considered by a provider in forming or choosing to participate in an IDS.

The various antitrust laws were enacted for the protection of competition. Current interpretations of antitrust restrictions in the health care field are sufficiently complex and burdensome as to have a chilling effect on the formation of integrated networks by providers. Knowledge of the general concerns driving antitrust regulators and case law is necessary to effective strategic planning. Antitrust counsel is necessary in the formation of many managed care arrangements.

Antitrust laws do not impede the full integration of a group of providers in a merger, provided that the merged entity does not possess market power sufficient to harm competition. On the other hand, many health care markets in the country are neither ready for nor suited for such complete integration, and interpretations of antitrust laws can have the effect of preventing the partial integration that many providers prefer when giving up their solo practices.

The primary area in which the antitrust laws create difficulties for individual practitioners or small provider groups is in the formation of relationships that fall short of full integration with providers who can be deemed "competitors." This situation arises when providers wish to form a group but maintain competitive practices outside of the network.

Acceptance of capitation and risk-withhold arrangements mitigates antitrust concerns (and will prevent antitrust scrutiny if the group represents less than 20% of its market). Discounted fee-for-service arrangements, on the other hand, raise concerns in any group negotiation. Federal regulators have approved the use of the somewhat cumbersome "messenger model" for negotiating price in such arrangements.

Under the messenger model, the practitioners appoint a third party to be the "messenger." The messenger communicates with each practitioner in the network individually to determine acceptable fee ranges. The messenger indicates to the payor which members have accepted. The FTC has recently made it clear that the messenger cannot actively negotiate and must act solely as a conduit of information to individual practitioners, the interests of both payors and providers in a more efficient process notwithstanding.

Partially integrated provider groups are thus prevented from entering bilateral negotiations. Such groups must clear two high hurdles before being able to engage in joint price negotiations with payors without incurring antitrust scrutiny. First of all, they must achieve sufficient integration, e.g., by accepting capitation arrangements or creating a new product that generates substantial efficiencies that are passed on to consumers. Second, even a legitimate joint venture must not represent too large a share of similar services in the market.

If a group requires exclusivity from its members, accounts for 20% or less of each specialty in a market, and is compensated through shared risk such as capitation and withhold arrangements, it will avoid scrutiny by the Justice Department and the Federal Trade Commission. Those joint ventures that do not fall within the safety zone will be analyzed according to traditional, but very complex and unpredictable, antitrust analysis. Many provider organizations choose to take their best shot at remaining within the safe harbor rather than venturing out on the treacherous open seas of antitrust review. A network representing more than 35% or 40% of any specialty in a market, especially if not paid on a capitation basis, may well be found to be illegal.

TAX STATUS

In forming a network, the decision must be made whether that entity will be conducted as for-profit or not-for-profit organization. For-profit entities have as a major objective financial returns for their investors. Conversely, not-for-profit organizations use their finances for stated public purposes. The decision of which status to pursue often drives network development—mission statements, bylaws, operational procedures, financial undertakings all hinge on this fundamental decision.

Both for-profit and not-for-profit organizations have their advantages and disadvantages, as outlined in Table 11. This information is provided as guidance in your decision making and should not be considered the rendering of legal advice. Legal and tax counsel must be consulted for guidance regarding state laws.

Taxable Organizations

Taxable organizations can be both for-profit and not-for-profit entities. In general, taxable organizations have fewer federal and state tax restrictions, which gives them greater flexibility in the areas of practitioner compensation, recruitment, and issues of ownership. Strengths and weaknesses of each organization are shown in Table 11.

TABLE 11 For-profit Verses Not-for-profit Taxable Organizations

FOR-PROFIT, TAXABLE INTEGRATED SYSTEMS

Entity Name	Strengths	Weaknesses
Corporation	• Limits shareholder liability • Dividend distribution to shareholders • No federal taxes on practitioner practice acquisition	• Taxed as an entity (potential for double taxation, particularly for shareholders—once for the corporate tax, once at federal and state) • Securities legal issues may develop • Investments of shareholders are at risk
Partnership	• No double taxation—partners taxed on partnership income	• IRS will scrutinize a tax-exempt entity that partners with private investors (practitioners) if the relationship crosses private benefit/private inurement lines • Partners become personally liable • Partners jointly liable for the practice • Any partner can create a liability case for the practice and other partners
Limited liability company	• Liability advantages of a corporation • Single-tax advantages of a partnership • Limits personal liability	• Relatively new organizational structure subject to state laws (vary by state)

NOT-FOR-PROFIT, TAXABLE ORGANIZATIONS

Not-for-profit taxable organization	• Income of corp. taxed at corporate rate • Shows sensitivity to cultural need for a non-profit entity • Simplifies governance • Avoids community benefit/private inurement restrictions	• Subject to federal *and* state taxes • "Members" rather than shareholders

Not-for-Profit, Tax-Exempt Organizations

Organizations that are formed and operated solely for charitable, educational, or scientific purposes are exempt from federal income tax by Section 501(c)(3) of the Internal Revenue Code as shown in Table 12. Provider mergers, a relatively new entity for the IRS, have come under increased scrutiny. The following issues are relevant to the formation of a network:

Benefits of tax-exempt, not-for-profit status:

- Exemption from federal corporate income tax
- Exemption from certain excise and unemployment taxes
- Access to low cost capital through the use of tax-exempt bonds (resulting in more favorable interest rates for the borrower)
- Organization may receive deductible contributions
- Possible exemption from state income taxes and local property taxes
- Exemption from price discrimination legislation
- Special postage rates for exempt organizations.

The IRS guideline for tax exemption requires fulfillment of all criteria in section 501(c)(3):

- *The system must be organized and operated solely for exempt purposes* (charitable purposes test and test for community benefit). Charitable includes relief of the poor and distressed, advancement of education and science, and/or the promotion of social welfare.
- *Net earnings are not paid, in any part, to the benefit of shareholders or an individual* (i.e., no private inurement).

The following "tests" for non-exemption are generally applied to a hospital for its tax-exemption. As of this writing, the Internal Revenue Service also applies the same standards to integrated health systems and has approved two California systems for tax-exemption. It appears that the IRS looks quite closely at all criteria, with a special emphasis on community benefit. *Note:* This material may be at a level of detail to be explored with competent legal counsel. However, as you develop an organization, the following tax issues should be kept in mind if you are considering a tax exemption (see also Figure 10):

1. Test for charitable purposes:
    - Do the organizing documents (charter, bylaws, articles of in-

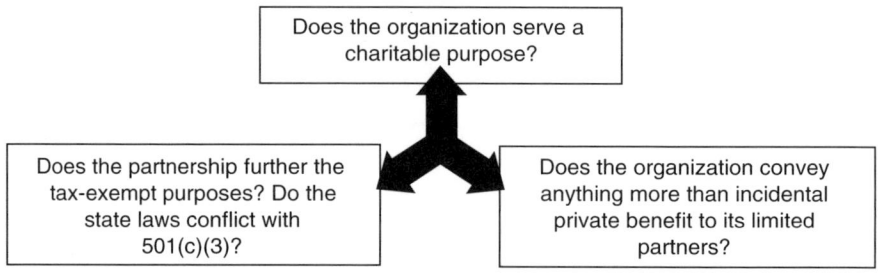

FIGURE 10 Tax exemption criteria.

corporation) generally set forth the charitable nature of the organization?
- Do the same documents limit the activities of the organization to those that further this charitable cause?

2. Test for community benefit:

A 1969 IRS ruling established that hospitals (or "systems" in this case) may claim tax-exemption on the basis of "promoting health" if it benefited the community. This precludes the need to provide absolute uncompensated care. The test for community benefit reads as follows:

- Does the system allow an open health care staff for qualified practitioners (consistent with the size and scope of services offered)?
- Does the system operate an emergency room and accept patients regardless of their ability to pay for services?
- Is the governing board composed of community members or community leaders?
- Does the system provide inpatient, non-emergency care and is it compensated through individual funds or third-party reimbursement (including Medicare and Medicaid)?
- Does the hospital lease available space in its medical building to members of the active medical staff?
- Although not technically required, the IRS tends to look favorably on organizations that offer research and public education as further proof of providing community benefit. Therefore, the network may want to develop a plan for publishing outcome studies as research.

3. Test for private inurement (qualitative/quantitative):

- Qualitative: Is the private inurement gained necessary to achieve the public benefit the organization seeks to achieve?
- Quantitative: Is the private benefit substantial when compared to the public benefit the organization seeks to achieve?

Steps to Obtaining Tax Exempt Status. **1.** *Submission of Form 1023.* This document includes information on the services to be offered, budget and financial information, governance, and articles of incorporation and bylaws. **2.** System *should be fully functional before 1023 submission.* This step is critical. Final negotiations for governance, asset acquisition, and compensation issues should be resolved. The organization could become operational before the IRS ruling as long as final documents are written to be flexible to IRS rulings or changes. **3.** Receive a *determination letter.* Since precedents are being set, the application will be likely sent to the IRS' national office for a case-by-case ruling.

GOVERNANCE STRUCTURE

In a recent ruling, the IRS imposed a "20% test" to the governance of integrated systems. Essentially, no more than 20% of the systems board can represent related health care groups and no more than 20% can have financial interests in foundation operations. Creative governance rules can work around this issue—such as restricted supermajority voting or restricted voting for members with financial interests.

TABLE 12   Not-for-profit, Tax-exempt Integrated Systems

Entity Name	Strengths	Weaknesses
Not-for-profit tax-exempt organization	• More consistent with existing hospital governance structures • Members not liable for corporation's conduct • Some states provide immunities to directors/officers • Corporate income is federally tax-exempt	• Owners maintain certain powers • No dividends distributed • Subject to rigorous IRS scrutiny for practitioner compensation and recruitment

The governance structure relates to the number and type of members on the governing body, usually referred to as the board of directors or trustees. Networks currently in operation usually have structured their board of directors in one of the following three forms:

- Equal representation by hospital and practitioner members. Voting is accomplished on a simple majority basis.
- Unequal representation on the board by one of the entities, usually the practitioners. Voting is accomplished on a simple majority basis.
- Unequal representation on the board by one of the entities, usually the practitioners. Voting on certain defined issues by a super majority vote. Voting on routine issues on a simple majority vote.

Equal Representation/Simple Majority

Under this board structure the parties to the network determine the number of board seats and each party gets an equal number of seats. All issues are voted on and a simple majority is needed to approve or disapprove a motion. There is usually no tie-breaker provision in this structure. See Table 13 for a summary of strenths and weaknesses.

Unequal Representation/Simple Majority

This board structure allows one party to have a majority of board members and therefore control the voting. This type of board structure is less common than the other structures and usually occurs when ownership of the network rests entirely with the hospital or the practitioners. The other situation when this type of board structure might occur is when the own-

TABLE 13 Equal Representation/Simple Majority

Strengths	Weaknesses
• Neither party has control over the other • Forces compromise and cooperation in order to accomplish the goals of the network	• Board members may reach an impasse on key issues that could be to the detriment of the network

TABLE 14 Unequal Representation/Simple Majority

Strengths	Weaknesses
• Decision making at the board level has less of a chance of reaching an impasse • Practitioners may feel less threatened by the integration process if they have control of the board	• Control by one party could lead to a feeling of frustration and mistrust by the minority party at not being able to significantly affect the outcome of board actions • Control by one party could lead to unequal treatment of the other party and prevent the board from considering issues from all points of view. This could hamper the future integration strategy of the network as it evolves.

ership of the network is split between the hospital and organized groups of primary care practitioners and separate groups of specialty practitioners. Each group would then have equal seats on the board, with practitioners as a whole having more seats. See Table 14 for a listing of strengths and weaknesses.

Unequal Representation/Super Majority

This type of board structure is sometimes referred to as a "consensus" board structure. In this structure, one party, usually the practitioners, has a larger number of board seats, but on certain issues a consensus of the majority of the board members representing each party is necessary to approve or disapprove a motion. The parties agree on which issues will require the super majority and which issues will require only a simple majority. This structure was initially developed to overcome the fear of many practitioners of being controlled by the hospital, while protecting the hospital's investment in the network. See Table 15 for a summary of strengths and weaknesses.

Community Representation

Some networks have decided to add business or community representatives to their boards to integrate the community into the health planning process and foster community input needed by the network. Alter-

TABLE 15 Unequal Representation/Super Majority

Strengths	Weaknesses
• Allows the practitioners a majority of the board seats and helps to overcome fear of control by the hospital • Routine decisions can be made quickly and without impasse • Forces both parties to compromise and cooperate on major issues affecting the network • Forces both parties to better understand each other's point of view	• Possible conflict between primary care and specialty practitioners on the number of seats each has on the board

natively, community and business input into the network can also be achieved by appointing a community advisory board as a committee of the board. The community advisory board has no authority to vote on issues before the network board, but they meet on a regular basis with the network board to discuss service issues and review new product options.

Unless a community representative is needed on the network board for legal or political reasons, the community advisory board concept is best suited for a new network. This will allow the practitioners and the hospital to strengthen their working relationship without outside interference, while still gaining vital community input.

OTHER LEGAL CONCERNS

Additional issues that may arise during the network's developmental phase include:

Credentialing and Peer Review

Networks may assume legal liability if screening and monitoring of practitioners is not sufficient to protect patients.

Employee Benefit Plans

The IRS may require employers comprising the network to be treated as a single employer for satisfying coverage, nondiscrimination, and ERISA

Among the array of services to be considered when starting a network are:

Specialty Services
- Adult mental behavioral health
- Adolescent mental behavioral health
- Child mental behavioral health
- Adult substance abuse
- Adolescent substance abuse

Continuum of Care Services
- Inpatient
- RTC
- Partial hospital programs
- Structured living for partial hospitalization
- Home health care
- Office care
- Half-way houses
- Behavioral health and wellness centers
- Community-based services

NETWORK HOSPITALS

The role of hospitals in networks is particularly complex because the success of the hospital may appear to be inversely related to the success of the network. Hospitals traditionally evaluate themselves in terms of average daily census or occupancy rates, two indicators the network must strive to reduce. There are simply too many acute-care hospital beds in the market. Some estimates are as high as 50% of the acute care beds are not necessary, and hospital downsizing must occur as an inevitable result of controlling utilization.

Realistic estimates of the number of acute-care beds needed per thousand lives must be made early in the network development stage. Affiliation with hospitals must be evaluated carefully to predict how well they can manage in a managed care environment. Hospitals with heavy debt, expensive infrastructures, and slowly responding leadership simply will not make good partners.

In fact, how a hospital partner will react to a declining census can not be reliably predicted. To the greatest extent possible, efforts should be made to modify hospital executives' definitions of success and to move their focus from revenue to margin, from census to discharges, from number of beds to number of lives.

Key Points in Picking Hospital Partners

- A start-up network should seek out hospital partners who already have shorter than average lengths of stay, have fewer employees per adjusted patient day, and have downsized their acute care operations to meet community needs.
- Hospitals must demonstrate in tangible ways that business has changed. Big buildings of brick and mortar are no longer the measure of a health care organization's success. Executives who continue to believe that bigger is better are not good partners in the managed care market environment. Discipline is required to down-size an organization, to prioritize needs, and stick to a budget. Providers with control of their overhead costs can drag down a network.

PROVIDERS

The single most difficult issue in network participation is the practitioner's loss of autonomy and control. Although some loss is inevitable, it can be minimized with careful planning and conscientious effort. One of the mechanisms for reducing the adverse effect of this loss is to engage practitioners in decision making. Some networks have effectively defined the responsibilities of the practitioner members and held their leadership accountable for producing results.

Key Points in Choosing Provider Members

- Does the practitioner enhance the network's delivery system (a needed specialty, geographic access or reputation)?
- No one is a better advocate for the network than a practitioner member. The quality improvement and utilization control systems they develop consistently out perform those developed by other staff members. Is the practitioner committed to the success of the network?
- In order for practitioners to participate in decision making, they must be able and willing to make the time commitment. Is the practitioner willing to make the commitment?

TABLE 16   Inclusion of a Range of Providers

Strength	Weakness
• A fully developed panel of providers may result in leverage to reduce costs by providing care at a lower level. For example, a visit with a clinical social worker may cost the network less than a session with a psychologist and meet the patient's needs equally well.	• The practitioner partners in the network may perceive the use of allied health professionals as a professional or quality threat.

- Holding practitioners accountable is extremely difficult. Many practitioners are very effective at resisting efforts to "manage" them. Will the practitioner actively support cost efficiency programs?

OTHER HEALTH CARE PROVIDERS

The network's decision regarding who to include on its provider panel may be dictated by state law. Exclusion of chiropractors, for example, may be prohibited by insurance regulations. Some states have adopted "any willing provider" clauses, which limit the network's exclusivity. See Table 16 for other factors to consider. The network is advised to evaluate the need for other health care providers in terms of customer expectations, state law, and the continuum of care. Among the providers to consider are:

- professional counselors
- certified psychiatric nurses
- clinical social workers
- community mental health centers
- psychiatrists
- marriage and family therapists

SUMMARY

Integration requires decisions to be made on the tax and legal structures to be adopted as well as defining the scope of services and governance of the network. Competent legal counsel may assist with these decisions.

CASE STUDY

At their next meeting, the practitioners review the results of their independent research to pursue development of a provider-driven delivery system. At Jim Moncrief's invitation, an attorney has joined them to explain what actions are likely to be prohibited under antitrust or Medicare's fraud regulations.

The attorney explains that, since they are planning to join together to form an equity model organization, they can collaborate without fear of antitrust action. What they cannot do is work together to set prices until the new organization is legally operational. Therefore, he suggests that they delay setting a fee schedule until the organizational structure is defined. He also explains that they cannot arbitrarily exclude a category of providers, like social worker, from participating in the organization. They do not have to be accepted as partners for equity purposes but cannot be "boycotted."

Carla Linden reports that, based upon her research, the organization can probably be set up as a limited liability partnership to avoid corporate taxes while protecting the members' personal assets. She advises against trying to secure tax-exemption as a not-for-profit organization because of the limits on private inurement and requirement to serve a charitable purpose.

Carla also raises the issue of how to partner with hospitals, physicians, and other providers in creating this organization. Cheryl suggests that they focus first on horizontal integration, joining together behavioral health practitioners and then consider approaching the physical health MSO with a plan to merge together. Cheryl points out that the MSO is planning to transition to an HMO within the year and that mental and behavioral health services could be a carve-out for the HMO.

The discussion of the continuum of care and scope of services to be offered results in a plan to develop an equity model IDS that includes all practitioner types, throughout the county, but to limit equity participation (partnership status) to psychologists and psychiatrists.

6

Infrastructure Needs for Integration

THE INFRASTRUCTURE NEEDED *to support a FIDS differs substantially from existing support for health care delivery. This chapter explores the administrative and clinical processes that must be developed and implemented for an IDS to be successful and cost efficient.*

ADMINISTRATIVE STRUCTURE

Space, staffing, and systems form the administrative infrastructure for the network. For the new network, two options appear very early in the process:

- Proceed with current space, staffing, and systems (e.g., borrowed from hospital or other partner), or
- Make significant capital and operating expenditures specifically to develop the network.

Physical Space

Many factors influence the decision about where to house the administrative offices of the network. Although office space may be immediately available inside the hospital, that location may convey a signal of hospital control. Additionally, as the staff grows, space demands will increase. Therefore, the location should be selected with future needs in mind.

Initially, basic space needs are limited to an office, reception area, and access to meeting space. By the end of the first year, approximately 3000 square feet of dedicated space may be necessary, depending on the size of

TABLE 17 Locating Network Offices in a Hospital

Strengths	Weaknesses
• As inpatient utilization declines, a patient wing can be converted to offices for the network • Access to hospital resources (e.g., fax, computer systems, copier, meeting rooms) will reduce start-up costs for the network • Access to borrowed personnel (e.g., UR coordinator, credentialing clerk) is convenient	• The perception of the medical community and the public will be that the network is "part of the hospital." Practitioners who are not affiliated with the hospital are unlikely to join the network. Conversely, hospital-affiliated practitioners who are not accepted into the network will resent their exclusion and may abandon the hospital • Although the space needs are limited during start-up, multiple relocations in one year are to be avoided because of the negative effect on staff morale, perceptions of commitment, and productivity

the administrative staff. The strengths and weaknesses (see Table 17) of locating the network offices in a hospital need to be considered before a decision is made. Although, this location may postpone some expenditures, the message it sends may offset the savings.

Staffing

The network does not need a large staff and the administrative burden of paying their salaries during the start-up period. Therefore, a minimalist approach to staffing is appropriate at first. The immediate requirements are:

- Director responsible for start-up
- Part-time secretary
- Consulting medical director

At least in the early years of the IDS's existence, legal and practice valuation consulting support will be necessary to permit the IDS to acquire existing practices and negotiate compensation agreements and other contractual arrangements. Local legal counsel is unlikely to offer the specialized expertise necessary during start-up but may work closely with outside counsel to gear up for future contract maintenance activities. Although a FIDS has a substantial advantage over other provider types in recruiting new practitioners at the beginning of their careers, retaining established practitioners who profess a preference for independent solo-practice may be a concern. Similarly, consulting assistance may be necessary for actuarial expertise, compensation arrangements, and medical management procedures. Additionally, the following skills may be "borrowed" from a network partner:

- Quality management advisor
- Financial advisor
- MIS support
- Credentialing support (medical staff coordinator)
- UR coordinator
- Marketing support

Provider Relations

For a network to be successful, it must recruit and retain a full panel of practitioners and other providers. This responsibility falls primarily to the provider relations staff. Although the administrator may fill this role during the initial stages of start-up, the network will soon need at least one person whose function it is to maintain communication with the provider panel to keep them abreast of current marketing initiatives, to explain utilization control processes, to research provider concerns, and to advocate on behalf of providers. Additionally, the provider relations staff will work closely with credentialing staff to add providers to the panel. Provider relations staff will expedite network growth.

Points to Consider in Choosing Provider Relations Staff:

- To the extent that existing relationships with the provider community can be leveraged, the network may want to hire hospital personnel who are already known to the hospital personnel. Hospital staff may make the transition to provider relations if they are highly respected by the clinical community.
- Existing relationships may reinforce the connection between the hospital and the new network. Recruiting provider relations staff

from outside the community may offer new insights and introductions to potential new network partners.

A key function of the provider relations group is education. Depending upon the prevalence of managed care contracting in the region, the network may be able to limit educational programs to those processes that differ from other existing networks; however, the network will be obliged to produce and distribute a provider manual containing a full description of its processes and procedures. Some networks issue new manuals at least annually to reduce their obsolescence and eliminate interfiling of updates. Others simply produce replacement pages for a loose-leaf manual. See Table 18 for some strengths and weaknesses of provider education methods.

Most networks also issue a quarterly newsletter to providers informing them of new members (i.e., new employer groups) and changes in procedures or referral specialist availability. One especially effective method for provider education is monthly luncheons for office and administrative staff. Hosted by the provider relations department, this routine session provides the practitioner office staff a forum for discussing problems and obtaining information. For the network, the forum offers an open communication channel for identifying and correcting problems.

Marketing Staff

The concept of integration was brought about by consumers' demand for more efficient and cost-effective methods of delivering health care services. Once providers have begun the process of creating a more efficient, cost-effective health care delivery system, the question becomes who to sell the services to? The market for network services ranges from self-

TABLE 18 Provider Education Strengths and Weaknesses

Strengths	Weaknesses
• Provider education programs permit provider staff to meet and communicate with network staff	• Manuals are often poorly organized, cumbersome, and not kept updated by network staff
• Provider manuals are reference tools for researching problems when claims reject or payment seems inadequate	• Manuals are expensive to produce and maintain. Office staff often discard or fail to interfile manual updates

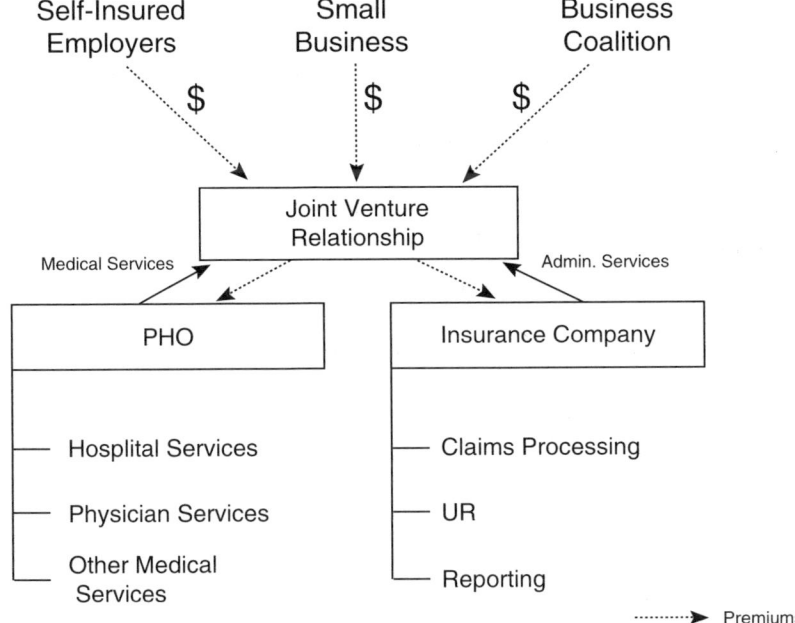

FIGURE 11 Network/Insurer joint venture relationship.

insured employers to insurance companies to other MCOs. Listed below is a listing of potential target markets that should be researched and prioritized:

- Local self-insured businesses
- Insurance carriers supplying health care coverage to local employers
- Small group carriers/local brokers

Insurance Carrier Partnership. Many networks are looking to form a partnership with large and small group insurance carriers who can supply needed administrative support (claims processing, marketing, etc.) and may find it attractive to contract with a ready-made network.

In mature integrated systems, joint venture relationships with insurance carriers and health care providers are becoming more common. Risk-sharing joint ventures are being formed to meet a variety of consumer needs. Figure 11 illustrates a joint venture relationship between a network and an insurer.

In this model, premiums are received from various organizations and distributed based on negotiated percentages to both parties. Each party then supplies those services it has expertise at to the health care purchaser.

Small Group/Insurer Partnership. Unlike the large employer market, many companies with fewer than 200 employees do not sponsor their own plans, but instead rely on insurance carriers to provide health benefits in compliance with applicable state laws. For many of these companies, total cost is the most important decision making criteria.

One increasingly popular strategy adopted by many networks as a means by which to attract this small group market segment is to partner with insurance companies who may commit necessary resources to aggressively market the network to the local business community. In this model, the insurer accepts most of the risk, with the network supplying services at a discounted rate and receiving a network access fee from the insurer. This model is illustrated in Figure 12.

These insurance carriers have trained actuaries and underwriters skilled in evaluating risk, maintain reserves (usually $1.25 million minimum) required by the states, have established distribution channels to market their products, and ample claims offices and administrative support services to analyze, price, market, and administer small group health plans.

Given the number of small businesses in the area and those without

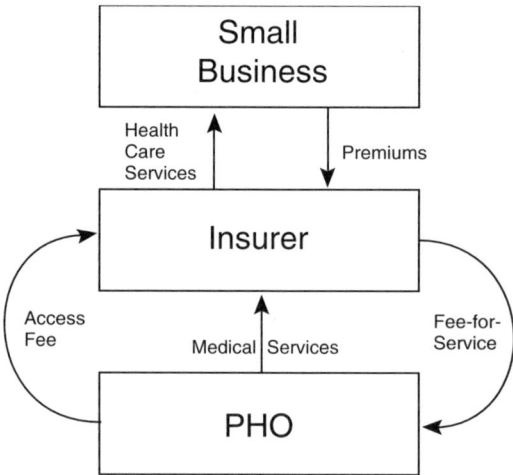

FIGURE 12   Small group/Insurer partnership.

health insurance, a partnership with the right carriers will provide the network with an opportunity to increase its volume of patients.

Although capitated reimbursement may be an option for future consideration, partnerships with small group carriers do not necessitate any risk bearing or sharing on the part of the network providers—another advantage to this approach.

The following outline provides a chronological sequence of the tasks that should be accomplished to successfully implement partnership arrangements with small group insurance carriers. However, the goals and objectives of the network, reimbursement methodologies, contracts and agreements with practitioners, organizational structure, utilization review and practice standards, claims repricing issues, access fees, member services, network directories, systems, and other related issues must first be identified and/or completed before any carrier can give the network serious consideration.

Task 1: Pre-qualify carriers through written questionnaires, phone interviews, and financial review. Select four to five carriers for live interviews.

Task 2: Interview selected prospective carriers for partnership potential. Analysis would include reputation, industry strength, experience in managed care, presence in the geographic area, and commitment of resources.

Task 3: Select two to three carrier partners to exclusively market the network to the local small business community.

Task 4: a. Provide hospital and practitioner reimbursement arrangements, rationale, and assumptions (including benefit plan design) to carriers for pricing analysis
b. Provide prototype contract to carriers for review
c. Provide network access fee alternatives
d. Provide draft copy of Network Provider Directory

Member Services

Just as the relationship of the network and providers must be managed, the network must have staff assigned to function as advocates for

68   PART II: HOW TO BUILD AN IDS

TABLE 19   Member Education Program Strengths and Weaknesses

Strengths	Weaknesses
• Educational efforts focus on specific membership needs can produce measurable results for the network • Health education materials may be considered "a cost of doing business" or promotional activities for a network	• General education programs are largely ineffective in changing behavior

members (i. e., the patients). These staff members need a broad, generalized knowledge of health care delivery and the managed care environment but must also be able to communicate clearly with the layperson in stressful situations and engage actively in problem solving.

Member services staff handle correspondence and telephone inquiries from members who require assistance with obtaining care or payment for care. They must understand utilization control processes but are not nurses. They must understand payment procedures but do not process claims.

In many networks, the skills of the member services staff determine the network's ultimate success, since stability and limiting turnover in membership rolls is a strong indicator of network profitability.

Points to Consider in Choosing Member Services Personnel:

- Hospital personnel are generally knowledgeable about health care delivery, especially in an acute care setting.
- Hospital staff may have difficulty communicating with members without sounding condescending. They may also have difficulty transferring allegiance from the clinical community to patient advocacy.

Additionally, most networks have developed an educational curriculum for members. See Table 19 for some strengths and weaknesses of such programs. Although a minimal fee is charged for attendance at these workshops, the fee may be waived upon referral from a practitioner. In other words, if a member is interested in stress control, a fee is charged for the class; if a practitioner sends the member to a stress reduction class, there is no fee.

During the initial start-up phase, some networks have simply subscribed to one of the commercially available health and wellness magazines on behalf of each member. Although the expense per member is sizable, it defers the need to invest immediately in staffing and developing in-house educational resources. After the membership has expanded, the costs may be examined as a trade-off.

CLINICAL MANAGEMENT

Monitoring health care delivery is a resource intensive task for the network. At least five distinct aspects of care must be monitored to assess quality:

- Customer satisfaction—surveys, complaint tracking
- Process—critical pathways, decision trees
- Outcomes—recidivism rates, return to work studies, effects of medication, type of treatment matched with psychosocial profile
- Appropriateness—pre-procedure review, second-opinion requirements
- Efficiency—cost studies, practitioner profiles / report cards

Many start-up networks contract out at least some portion of developing the systems and processes necessary to monitor care. UM criteria and standards may be purchased from InterQual or adopted from the State Professional Review Organization (PRO). Quality management criteria must include, at a minimum, NCQA's HEDIS standards, which are summarized in this section.

The strengths and weaknesses of purchasing a UR system are listed in Table 20.

TABLE 20 Pros and Cons of Purchasing a UR System

Strengths	Weaknesses
• Immediate implementation of full tracking system • Low investment of time and resources • Nationally recognized standards that do not perpetuate local behavior patterns • Less political influence on decisions	• Less "buy-in" on standards and criteria • May encourage "we" versus "they" attitudes • Less control over process

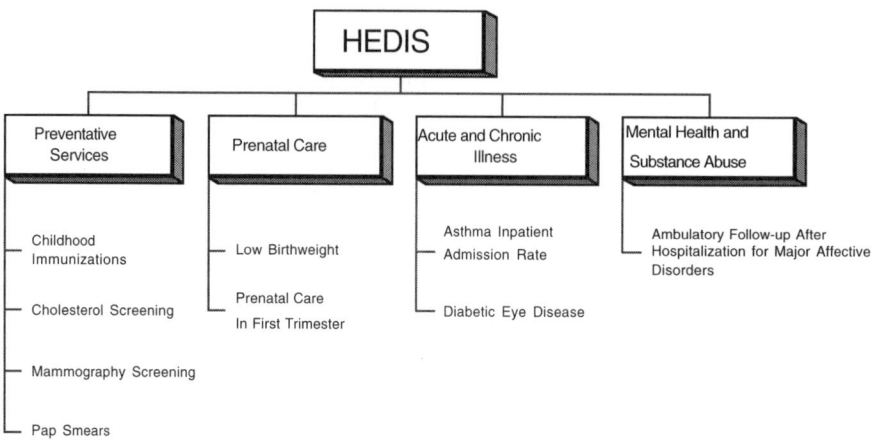

FIGURE 13 HEDIS quality measurement variables.

HEDIS is a data set allowing employers/purchasers of managed care plans to evaluate health plan *performance* and *value*. *Developed* by a coalition of HMOs and employers, HEDIS seeks to hold providers accountable for quality of care as well as to allow "apples to apples" comparison across different plans. Measurement is the cornerstone of HEDIS and includes indicators for clinical outcome, access to care, membership and utilization, patient satisfaction, and financial security.

HEDIS utilizes four distinct groups in measuring a managed care program's outcomes and quality performance. These groups include preventive services, prenatal care, acute and chronic illness, and mental behavioral health and substance abuse. Within each grouping, HEDIS specifically identifies and defines a total of nine quality measures, as depicted in Figure 13.

INFORMATION SYSTEMS

A plan member arrives without an appointment at the neighborhood clinic complaining of headache and dizziness. At the reception desk, she swipes her membership card against the magnetic reader or keys in her social security number on the key pad if she prefers. Within a few moments a nurse calls her from the waiting room to the triage area, where her vital signs and symptoms are recorded into the clinical system, which alerts the triage nurse that the patient's hypertension medication is awaiting pick up at the pharmacy. Accordingly, the "expert" system suggests appropriate questions to determine patient compliance with the medication regime prescribed. Once the patient's responses are recorded, the clinic physician reviews the information on-line and orders into the system or decides to examine the patient. Because of patient non-compliance with treatment protocol, the patient is scheduled for an appointment with the appropriate behavioral health practitioner for evaluation and treatment in accordance with an established protocol for non-compliance. At the end of the month, profile reports indicate that the patient's primary care physician (PCP) has a higher than average incidence of patient non-compliance. The physician receives this information and develops an action plan for improving patient compliance (in this case, taking the time to require the patient to voice a commitment and reasons for compliance). Improved results are demonstrated the following month and the physician receives the profile data electronically to provide positive feedback and confirm improvement.

This scenario is hardly science fiction. Key pads, swipe cards, clinical information systems, practice profiles, and e-mail systems already exist. What are missing are the linkages necessary to tie them together purposefully to improve health care delivery. Many hospitals have already begun implementing clinical support or "expert" systems to alert practitioners of abnormal findings, drug interactions, and diagnostic decision trees; however, systems suitable for the outpatient clinic setting have been slow to develop because of the overwhelming prevalence of small groups and solo-practitioners. With the emergence of large multi-specialty groups and IPAs, real-time clinical systems permit practitioners on-line access to the patient's history with all providers and in all settings, encourage compliance with treatment protocols established by the IDS, and facilitate profiling and data aggregation.

In other words, a sophisticated computer network is a critical infrastructure issue for any IDS. Among the key systems capabilities and features are:

- on-line real-time access
- membership data
- clinical patient history (on-line medical record)
- aggregated clinical information
- communications (e-mail) support
- protocol alerts (expert)
- statistical analysis (variance identification)

In particular, the IDS must be able to administer incentive mechanisms that encourage a service or customer-oriented attitude among all practitioners. The IDS must avoid poor service or bureaucratic images. One method for accomplishing this goal is increased automation of clerical procedures to expedite patient processing without reducing the personal attention to patients.

Current trends over the last twenty years have been to purchase information systems. Purchased systems offer the flexibility of regional databases that can be customized for your data. Additionally, they are flexible enough to accept data in various forms (tape and diskette most commonly). Regional databases make retrieval of information fast and convenient for most users. Purchased systems typically also allow for standard and customized reports and are capable of interfacing with many transaction systems.

Costs for management information systems (MISs) typically depend on the complexity of the required reporting capability. Consider the costs shown in Table 21 as "ballpark" figures—actual costs may be more or less depending on requirements and need for technical support.

TABLE 21   Costs For Management Information Systems

Multi-functional, micro-computer single-user system	• Up to $60,000
Mainframe computer—same system as above	• Up to $125,000
Network software	• Variable, negotiate continuous upgrades to the system to ensure the system will grow with the organization
Maintenance fees (software upgrades, telephone hotline, enhancements)	• 1 to 1.5% of installed software fees per month
Likely additional costs	• Installation • Training • Manual conversion work (i.e., loading contracts) • Consulting/accounting assistance in developing cost standards and verifying MIS results

Implementation

In general, networks can expect 3 to 6 months from the beginning of the project to generation of "production" reports. There is no appreciable difference in time to implementation between microcomputers and mainframes.

Implementation processes vary greatly depending on the level of vendor support. Plan for two full-time analysts during the process to analyze and validate system results. Expect to be billed for vendor on-site work by technicians. On-site support should be negotiated with the vendor and considered in the selection of a system.

Maintenance:
- *Periodic requirements*
  Spot-checking validity of reports
  Updating contracts "X" times per month
  Review for "reasonableness" of the output
- *Other*
  Enter new managed care contracts as they come available
- *Options for maintenance requirements*
  Hire a full-time analyst
  Contract with the vendor for analytical support (can be done on a capitated basis)

BUDGET PROJECTIONS

The network will need to generate sufficient revenue to cover its operating expenses in the long term. This revenue will be generated from both internal and external sources.

Many networks charge an annual membership fee to the practitioner and hospital members of the network. With the IPA currently in place, a portion of the dues paid to the IPA could be allocated to the network, if the practitioners desire. Network membership fees could still be collected from non-IPA practitioners if they are allowed to join the network. The hospital(s) in the network could also be charged a yearly membership fee.

Another internal source of revenue option is to charge a flat fee per patient visit or inpatient day for all patients treated through network contracts. This system attempts to charge for the network's services based on the provider receiving the benefit (patients) from the network.

External sources of revenue for the network usually come from the collection of access fees from employers, insurance carriers, and other MCOs. Recently, though, many MCOs and employers have refused to pay access fees. Their refusal is usually linked to their ability to purchase services from alternate providers other than the network. In some cases, networks have been able to negotiate per diem or per discharge rates with an MCO that included an additional amount to cover the administrative costs of the network. The degree to which external sources of revenue are available will largely depend on the negotiating strength of the network.

If the network accepts capitated per member per month premiums, a piece of that premium is set aside to cover the network's administrative costs. This percentage is usually 8% to 15% of the monthly premium.

As staffing needs grow during the first year, the administrative budget will rapidly expand from as low as $20,000 per month to over $150,000 per month. To a certain extent, administrative and consulting expenses may be seen as a trade-off. As staffing expenses grow, reliance on consultants should decline. However, educational expenses for newly hired employees may also be high.

THIRD PARTY ADMINISTRATION

Once the network is operational, expenses for computer processing and other operating functions will grow quickly. One approach is to contract with a third party administrator (TPA) for support of operational activities.

TPAs contract on either a paid claims, a processed claim, or a capitated basis for their services. Some TPAs have been accused of inflating the processed claim count by delaying or denying claims, which results in resubmissions and higher numbers of claims. This possibility may be avoided by contracting on a paid claims basis; however, for a new network, the capitated rate may be the best method since it produces a "no-surprises" budget. In general, operating expenses will vary from $5 to $15 per member per month dependent upon the services included in the contract.

OUTSIDE ASSISTANCE

Almost all networks use consultants to perform specialized services such as actuarial analysis of costs and production of rate manuals, due diligence review of contracts, and financial accounting. Some networks utilize consultants extensively during the start-up phase to postpone hiring staff to perform network development. For a network that elects to fully utilize consulting assistance, the budget may total $300,000 or more. Among the optional activities that may be performed by consultants are:

- guiding development of a strategic plan
- establishing organizational structure for the network
- developing policies and procedures for utilization control, quality management, and credentialing
- developing provider and member handbooks
- developing marketing materials
- performing vendor selection for TPA, UR, and quality measurement services
- negotiating contracts with providers, MCOs, and employers
- recruiting, selecting, and training staff
- assisting with preparations for NCQA survey

As discussed previously, the consulting and administrative budgets may be viewed as trade-offs. All of the start-up functions must be performed in order for the network to succeed. To the extent that local expertise can be identified and recruited quickly and efficiently, it should be utilized instead of a consultant; however, time is often short during start-up, and negotiating an employment contract is time consuming.

During start-up, the network will also incur substantial legal expenses for articles of incorporation, organizational structure, contract review and negotiation, and due diligence review of credentialing, grievance, and peer review policies.

Many networks obtain the services of an attorney specializing in health care to assist their local firm, which functions under retainer. The local attorney serves as a channel to the specialist, assisting network staff to frame specific questions so that the specialist's time is efficiently utilized. Additionally, the local attorney maintains an audit trail and control file for documentation purposes. The network's local attorney will also be performing duties such as structuring employment contracts, leases, and other more typical business arrangements. Typical legal expenses for the first year may well exceed $100,000, depending on the size of groups. Some networks, on the other hand, rely upon the hospital's legal counsel for assistance and incur substantially reduced expenses.

CASE STUDY

The next meeting of the practitioners is led by Mike Byrd, who has developed a plan for start-up of the organization. Mike suggests that once the organization has been legally formed, they will need to hire an administrator to "make things happen." Hiring an administrator will require renting an office, which will require a capital commitment by the partners.

Although the tone of this meeting is less enthusiastic than their others, the partners agree to invest in the organization to get it started. Carla agrees to function as interim president, and her office manager will be an interim administrator until one can be recruited. Cheryl and her staff will function as the "marketing department" for the organization, recruiting additional partners. Mike agrees to serve as treasurer and set up a bank account for the organization. Jim will continue as liaison with the legal counsel and focus on drafting a set of bylaws, rules, and other documents necessary for the legal structure.

Each partner also agrees to an initial investment of $3000 as start-up capital. For the next three months, each new partner will be required to contribute $4000. After that, each new partner will contribute $5000 capital.

Mike will continue his efforts to identify an investor who will handle the start-up costs of the organization. In particular, he has scheduled a meeting with the physical health MSO to investigate their willingness to help.

Glossary

ACCESS Patients' ability to obtain needed health services. Measures of access include the location of health facilities and their hours of operation, patient travel time and distance to health facilities, the availability of medical services, and the cost of care.

AVERAGE LENGTH OF STAY (ALOS) Number of days a patient customarily remains an inpatient for a specified diagnosis or procedure; used in precertification and recertification procedures.

CAPITATION A method of payment for health care services in which the provider accepts a fixed amount of payment per subscriber, per period of time, in return for providing specified services over a specified period of time.

CARVE OUT An arrangement in which coverage for a specific category of services (e.g., mental behavioral health/substance abuse, vision care, prescription drugs) is provided through a contract with a separate set of providers. The contract with these providers may specify certain payment and utilization management arrangements.

CASE MANAGEMENT The monitoring, planning, and coordination of treatment rendered to patients with conditions expected to require high cost or extensive services. Case management is focused and longitudinal, usually following the member for 3–6 months minimum to avoid readmission.

CASE MANAGER A generic term for various professionals who perform different case management functions, usually working with clients, families, providers, and insurers to coordinate all services deemed necessary to provide the client with a plan of medically necessary and appropriate health care.

CHANNEL A frequent referral source.

CONCURRENT REVIEW A third-party review of the medical necessity, level of care, length of stay, appropriateness of services, and discharge planning for patients in health care facilities. Occurs at the time the patient is being treated.

CONTINUUM OF CARE   In behavioral health, generally defined as the spectrum of care delivered in residential treatment, inpatient, partial hospitalization, home health, and outpatient settings.

COST CONTAINMENT   Actions taken by employers and insurers to curtail health care costs, e.g., increasing employee cost sharing, requiring second opinions, or preadmission screening.

COST SHARING   Requirement that health care consumers contribute to their own medical care costs through deductibles and coinsurance or copayments.

CREDENTIALING   The process of reviewing a practitioner's training, experience, and demonstrated ability for the purpose of determining if criteria for clinical privileging are met.

DISCHARGE PLANNING   Process of identifying, monitoring, counseling, and arranging follow-up care of hospitalized patients. Usually performed by case managers, social workers, or nurses, the process ensures patients receive appropriate counseling and follow-up care to assist their convalescence and keep hospital stays at a minimum.

FEE FOR SERVICE   In the traditional fee for service model, the provider bills the consumer or payer for a specified amount, typically on the basis of the amount of time spent delivering the service. Until recently, the provider determined the fee charged for the service and customary fees were generally accepted. Now, the provider may be required to accept a payer's fee schedule, which demands a certain fee be accepted as payment in full. PPOs represent an attempt to save the fee for service method of payment by regulating the cost of treatment in the context of a traditional reimbursement plan.

FEE SCHEDULE   A listing of accepted fees or predetermined monetary allowances for specified services and procedures.

FREE-STANDING FACILITY   A health care center that is physically separated from a hospital or other institution of which it is a legal part or with which it is affiliated, or an independently operated or owned private or public business or enterprise providing a limited health care service or range such as ambulatory surgery, hemodialysis treatment, diagnostic tests or examinations, etc.

GATEKEEPING   The process by which a primary care provider directly provides the primary patient care and coordinates all diagnostic testing and specialty referrals required for a patient's medical care. Referrals must be prior-authorized by the "gatekeeper" unless there is an emergency. Gatekeeping is a subset of the functions of the primary provider case manger.

GROUP MODEL HMO   An HMO that contracts with a primary care or multi-specialty group practice for the delivery of health services.

GROUP PRACTICE   The organization of a group of practitioners as a private partnership, limited liability company, or corporation; participating practitioners share facilities and personnel as well as earnings from their practice. The providers comprising the practice may represent either a single specialty or a range of behavioral health specialties.

HEALTH MAINTENANCE ORGANIZATION (HMO)   A health care delivery system that provides comprehensive health services to an enrolled population, frequently for a prepaid, fixed (capitated) payment although other payment arrangements can be made. The organization consists of a network of health care providers rendering a wide range of health services and assumes the financial risk of providing these services. Enrollees generally will not be reimbursed for care provided outside the HMO network.

INDEMNITY INSURANCE PLAN   An insurance plan that pays specific dollar amounts to the insured individual for specific services and procedures without guaranteeing complete coverage for the full cost of health care services.

INDIVIDUAL PRACTICE ASSOCIATION (IPA)   An organization that unites individual health care professionals to provide services in their own offices under contract. The specialists are generally paid on a fee-for-service basis, but primary care providers may receive capitated payments.

INTEGRATED CARE   An alternative delivery system developed by the American Psychological Association as a response to the rising costs of providing health care services. Based on six concepts: Benefit design, case management and utilization review, communications, direct contracting, network development, and outcomes.

INTEGRATED DELIVERY SYSTEM (IDS)   A system of behavioral health care offering "one-stop shopping" to potential payers, meaning that a payer can write one check for the entire delivery of behavioral health care without having to independently negotiate terms with multiple, unconnected providers. IDSs offer a full continuum of care so that the patients and premiums are managed within one accountable plans' network of providers.

LEVERAGE   A managed care strategy for controlling costs by steering patients to lower cost providers called substitutes. In behavioral health care, a clinical social worker or psychiatric nurse may be a substitute for a psychologist.

MANAGED CARE   A means of providing health care services within a defined network of health care providers who are given the responsibility to manage and provide quality, cost-effective care. Increasingly, the term is being used by many analysts to include (in addition to HMOs), PPOs and even forms of indemnity insurance coverage that incorporate preadmission certifications and other utilization controls.

MARKET SHARE   That part of the market potential that a managed care company has captured, usually market share is expressed as a percentage of the market potential.

MANAGEMENT SERVICES ORGANIZATION (MSO)   An entity that usually contracts with practitioner groups, IPAs, and medical foundations to provide a range of services required in medical practices, such as accounting, utilization review, and staffing.

MULTISPECIALTY GROUP   A group of doctors who represent various specialties and who work together in a group practice.

NETWORK   A group of providers that mutually contract with carriers or employers to provide health care services to participants in a specified managed care plan. The contract determines the payment method and rates, utilization controls, and target utilization rates by plan participants.

NETWORK MODEL   An organizational form in which the HMO contracts for medical services within a "network" of medical groups. HealthNet, a Blue Cross sponsored HMO serving southern California, is an example of a network model. For federal qualification purposes, such models are designated as IPAs.

PEER REVIEW   Evaluation by practicing providers (or other qualified professionals) of the quality and efficiency of services ordered or performed by other practicing providers. Peer review is the all-inclusive term for medical review efforts. Medical practice, inpatient hospital, and extended care facility analyses, utilization review, medical audit, ambulatory care, and claims review are all aspects of peer review.

PERFORMANCE STANDARDS   Standards an individual provider is expected to meet, especially with respect to quality of care. The standards may define volume of care delivered per time period.

PREADMISSION REVIEW   When a provider requests that a patient be hospitalized, another opinion may be sought. The second provider reviews the treatment plan and evaluates the patient's condition, and confirms the request for admission or recommends another course of action. Similar to second opinions on surgery.

PREAUTHORIZATION   Review and approval of covered benefits, based on a provider's treatment plan. Some insurers require preauthorization for certain high cost procedures. Other insurers apply the preauthorization requirement when charges are in excess of a specified dollar amount.

PRECERTIFICATION   A review of the necessity and length of a recommended hospital stay. Certification prior to admission is often required for all non-emergencies and certification within 48 hours following admission for emergency treatment.

PREEXISTING CONDITION   Any condition for which charges have been incurred during a specified period of time just prior to the effective date of an insurance policy. Frequently, a contract with a different insurer will not cover the preexisting conditions of employees or their dependents.

PREFERRED PROVIDER ORGANIZATION (PPO)   Selective contracting agreement with a specified network of health care providers at reduced or negotiated payment rates. In exchange for reduced rates, providers frequently receive expedited claims payment and/or a reasonably predictable market share. Employees have financial incentives to utilize PPO providers.

PROVIDER   Any health care professional (or facility) licensed to provide one or more health care services to patients.

PROVIDER HOSPITAL ORGANIZATION (PHO)   A vertically integrated delivery system formed by practitioners and a hospital.

QUALITY ASSURANCE   Activities and programs intended to ensure the quality of care in a defined medical setting or program. Such programs include methods for documenting clinical practice, educational components intended to remedy identified deficiencies in quality, as well as the components necessary to identify and correct such deficiencies (such as peer or utilization review), and formal process to assess the program's own effectiveness.

QUALITY MANAGEMENT   A participative intervention in which all employees and managers continuously review the quality of the service they provide. The process used identifies problems, tests solutions to those problems, and constantly monitors the solutions for improvement.

RISK   The chance or possibility of loss. The sharing of risk is often employed as a utilization control mechanism within the HMO setting. Risk is often defined in insurance terms as the possibility of loss associated with a given population.

RISK POOL   A pool of money that is to be used for defined expenses. Commonly, if the money that is put at risk is not expended by the end of the year, some or all of it is returned to those managing the risk.

SEAMLESS   A desired characteristic of a delivery system defined by the lack of gaps in the continuum of care.

SELECTIVE CONTRACTING   Negotiation by third party payers of a limited number of contracts with health care professionals and facilities in a given service area. Preferential reimbursement practices and/or benefits are then offered to patients seeking care from these providers.

SELF FUNDING   A procedure whereby a firm uses its own funds to pay claims, rather than transferring the financial risks of paying claims to an outside insurer in exchange for premium payment. Also referred to as self-insurance. Insurance companies and other third party administrator organizations may be engaged to process claims or the self-insured company may choose to handle its own. Four forms of claims administration are common:

COST PLUS   Third party pays claims and bills the employer for the actual amount of claims in a month (cost) plus an administrative fee to a carrier (plus).

ADMINISTRATIVE SERVICES ONLY (ASO)   Employer contracts with a firm to handle claims and make payments for billed services.

SELF-ADMINISTRATION   Employer takes on the risk for claims and does the administrative work involved in paying claims.

MINIMUM PREMIUM PLAN   Insurance company provides aggregate stop-loss protection plus claims adminstration services.

STAFF MODEL HMO   An HMO in which professional providers within a multispecialty group are salaried employees of the HMO.

STOP-LOSS COVERAGE   Insurance for a self-insured plan that reimburses the company for any losses it might incur in its health claims beyond a specified amount.

Substitute   An alternative provider who may replace another in spite of differences in training and licensing scope. A clinical social worker and a psychiatric nurse may be substitutes.

Third Party Administrator (TPA)   Outside company responsible for handling claims and performing administrative tasks associated with health insurance plan maintenance.

Third Party Payer   Any organization that pays or insures health care expenses on behalf of beneficiaries or recipients who pay premiums for such coverage.

Usual, Customary, and Reasonable (UCR)   Health insurance plans that pay a provider's full charge if it is reasonable and does not exceed his or her usual charges and the amount customarily charged for service by other providers in the area.

Utilization Review (UR)   An independent determination of whether health care services are appropriate and medically necessary on a prospective, concurrent, and/or retrospective basis to ensure that appropriate and necessary health care services are provided. UR is frequently used to curtail the provision of inappropriate services and/or to ensure that services are provided in the most cost-effective manner.

Value Based Purchasing   Selection of a product or service on criteria other than unit price. Value criteria may include quality, outcome, and access as well as cost.

Bibliography

Allen, D.W. (1993). Planning for the future of behavioral health services. *Health Care Strategic Management, 11*(10),16–19.

Aust, M.E. (1992). Regional model continues to grow in popularity. *Medical Group Management Journal, 39*(4), 44–64.

Bohlmann, R.C. (1995). The state of integration: today and tomorrow. *Medical Group Management Journal, 42*(1), 24–29.

Braun, J.L. (1995). MSOs: Key to PHOs and Community-Based Health Care Systems. *Physician Executive, 21*(2), 28–29.

Cerne, F. (1993). Benefits equity: providers anticipate core mental behavioral health coverage. *Hospitals, 67*(8),40–41.

DeMuro, P.R. (1994). Integrated delivery systems. *Topics in Health Care Financing, 20*(3),1–81.

England, M.J. & Cole, R.F. (1992). Building systems of care for youth with serious mental illness. *Hospital and Community Psychiatry, 43*(6), 630–633.

Fine, A. (1994). *Integrated health care delivery systems: A guide to successful strategies for hospital and physicians collaboration,* 1994. New York: Thompson.

Goldberg, R.J. & Fogel, B.S. (1989). Integration of general hospital psychiatric services with freestanding psychiatric hospitals. *Hospital and Community Psychiatry, 40*(10), 1057–1061.

Goldstein, D. (1995). On assignment. *Health Care Strategic Management, 13*(1), 6.

Harris, M. & Bergman, H.C. (1988). Capitation financing for the chronic mentally ill: A case management approach. *Hospital and Community Psychiatry, 39*(1), 68–72.

Hill, T.J. (1992). A catalyst for cooperation. *Medical Group Management Journal, 39*(5), 39–41.

Integrated delivery systems need consistent checkups. (1994). *Medical Network Strategy Report, 3*(12),1–3.

Johnson, B.A. & Schryver, D.L. (1994). Positioning for vertical integration through clinics "without walls". *Medical Group Management Journal, 41*(3), 80–84.

Jones, K. (1992). Interest in "group without walls" continues to grow. *Medical Group Management Journal, 39*(4), 36–38.

Lehman, A.F. (1989). Strategies for improving services for the chronic mentally ill. *Hospital and Community Psychiatry, 40*(9), 916–920.

Main, D.C. (1993). *Forming physician networks.* Chicago: American Medical Association.

Mechanic, D. (1994). Integrating mental behavioral health into a general health care system. *Hospital and Community Psychiatry, 45*(9), 893–897.

Mechanic, D. (1991). Strategies for integrating public mental behavioral health services. *Hospital and Community Psychiatry, 42*(8), 797–801.

Middletown's renaissance. (1994). *Hospitals & Health Networks, 68*(20), 6.

Murphy, T.M. & Hardy, C.T. (1994). *Hospital physician integration strategies for success.* Chicago: American Hospital.

Neiderman, G.A. & Johnson, B.A. (1994). Integrated provider networks—a primer. *Medical Group Management Journal, 41*(6), 62–68.

Okin, R.L. & Dolnick, J. (1985). Beyond state hospital unitization: The development of an integrated mental behavioral health management system. *Hospital and Community Psychiatry, 36*(11), 1201–1205.

Organized systems of care: A vision of a future healthcare delivery system. (1992). *Health Progress, 73*(8), 22–28.

Provan, K.G. & Milward, H.B. (1994). Integration of community-based services for the severely mentally ill and the structure of public funding: A comparison of four systems. *Journal of Health Politics, Policy and Law, 19*(4), 865–894.

Second stage of managed care will shift power to physicians. (1995). *Physician's Managed Care Report, 3*(3), 25–30.

Taylor, K.S. (1994). Benefit equity: Mental behavioral health providers want a place along the continuum. *Hospitals & Health Networks, 68*(9), 44+.

Trace, K. (1995). Practical guidelines for group practice integration. *Health Care Strategic Management, 13*(3), 12–13.

Vogel, D.E. (1993). *The physician and managed care.* Chicago: American Medical Association.

Williams, L. (1993). *The physician's role in the development of physician hospital organizations.* Chicago: American Medical Association.